Academic Transformation

PRAISE FOR ACADEMIC TRANSFORMATION

"Malm and Weber's new book provides a much-needed focus on the 'New Majority' of students in our colleges and universities. The authors include in the New Majority both adult students and the 18- to 22-year old with significant life responsibilities. If you are a university administrator, faculty member, or staff member, read this book and give it to your teams to read and discuss. It will help you adapt to the new reality of the students we serve."
—Marie Cini, senior research fellow and former provost, University of Maryland, University College

"The adult learner is a significant part of our undergraduate populations today, and it is critical that colleges and universities recognize them and their distinct needs. This book provides some helpful perspectives on how colleges need to think about their programs to make sure that they are meeting the needs of a student population that is not coming to college right out of high school."
—Becky Klein-Collins, associate vice president of research and policy development, Council for Adult and Experiential Learning (CAEL)

"This two-book series is a major step forward in addressing the demographic changes affecting post-secondary education. The series offers an innovative framework for re-thinking who the traditional student is, as well as strategies to create institutional changes to establish effective learning environments for the 'New Majority' of adult learners. Drs. Malm and Weber have used their extensive experience in higher education to create this timely and important series. I strongly believe that faculty and administrators from across the university community will find this an invaluable resource for creating more inclusive environments for today's diverse student body."
— Christy M. Rhodes, AAACE 2017 conference chair and assistant professor, interdisciplinary professions, East Carolina University

Academic Transformation

A Design Approach for the New Majority

Edited by Eric Malm
and Marguerite Weber

ROWMAN & LITTLEFIELD
Lanham • Boulder • New York • London

Published by Rowman & Littlefield
A wholly owned subsidiary of The Rowman & Littlefield Publishing Group, Inc.
4501 Forbes Boulevard, Suite 200, Lanham, Maryland 20706
www.rowman.com

Unit A, Whitacre Mews, 26-34 Stannary Street, London SE11 4AB

Copyright © 2018 by Eric Malm and Marguerite Weber

All rights reserved. No part of this book may be reproduced in any form or by any electronic or mechanical means, including information storage and retrieval systems, without written permission from the publisher, except by a reviewer who may quote passages in a review.

British Library Cataloguing in Publication Information Available

Library of Congress Cataloging-in-Publication Data Available

978-1-4758-3603-5 (cloth : alk. paper)
978-1-4758-3604-2 (pbk. : alk. paper)
978-1-4758-3605-9 (electronic)

∞™ The paper used in this publication meets the minimum requirements of American National Standard for Information Sciences Permanence of Paper for Printed Library Materials, ANSI/NISO Z39.48-1992.

Printed in the United States of America

Contents

Acknowledgments		vii
Preface		ix
1	An Introduction to the New Majority *Eric Malm*	1
2	The Pragmatic Mind-Set of New Majority Students *Ayisha Sereni*	13
3	Providing Student-Centered Support for Adult Students *Patricia Griffin*	23
4	Fit-Fear-Focus: Developing Learners' Sense of Belonging, Security, and Hope *Marguerite Weber*	35
5	Technology: Higher-Education Disruption and New Majority–Learner Access *Paul Walsh*	49
6	Program and Course Design for the New Majority *William A. Egan*	59
7	The Financial Dimension: Institutional Readiness for New Majority Learners *Eric Malm and Marguerite Weber*	73
8	Learning with Others: Working with Others to Build the New Majority Institution: An Interview with Dr. Eric Malm and Dr. Marguerite Weber *Beverly Schneller*	85
References		97
About the Editors		101
About the Contributors		103

Acknowledgments

A few years ago I started to become more aware of the complex lives that many of my students lead and was challenged to find ways to leverage their work and outside experiences to help them learn more about business disciplines. Their complex lives could either help or hurt their classroom learning. There was little discussion about these challenges on campus, and for some time I didn't make connections to the world of "adult education," or similar labels because most of my students appeared to be traditionally aged.

Then Dr. Marguerite Weber came to our campus community to help develop a degree-completion program for working adult learners. Soon our paths crossed. Intrigued by what she was doing, I suddenly found a language to describe much of what I was observing and discovering in the classroom. We came to call this set of students the *New Majority* and our conversations eventually resulted in this book.

As I learned about the literature on adult and nontraditional students, it was heartening to know that many of my instincts as a teacher connected to known issues and strategies for adult learners. Consistent with national trends, the lives of my students are increasingly complex. As I became more aware of that complexity, it became easier and more comfortable to restructure classes and approaches around changing needs. I also benefitted from conversations with colleagues from the "adult education space"—several of whom are contributors to this book—about the good work in this area that many people have been doing for years.

The writing of this book would not have been possible without the participation and support of many people. My provost, dean, and department chair were supportive of the project, and I was granted a sabbatical to pursue it. The project would not have been possible without the work contributors and other colleagues. Most importantly, I'd like to thank all the New Majority students out there who continue to find ways of balancing work and life and help professors and institutions transform to meet the needs of our students.

Eric Malm

I've had the great privilege of teaching a wide range of students for thirty-two years, and my first words of gratitude must go to the students who have been so generous with teaching me. Dr. Beverly Schneller, a great colleague and true friend, contributed so much to this work, which would not have come together as well without her wise counsel, boundless talent, and enormous good will. My husband Roger has given me such kind support. As a talented second-career professor himself, he has taught me much about becoming an entrepreneurial leader. From the days long ago when my young toddler Claire sat on my lap while I tried to bang out a dissertation to today, her fierce pride in me has been my constant joy. Finally, I'd like to thank Dr. Martha "Marty" Smith, former president of Anne Arundel Community College. When I was just starting in this profession, she was my mentor and role model. She gave me opportunities and encouragement, and I have always thought of my debt to her as I have tried, in whatever measure I could, to pay it forward.

Marguerite Weber

Preface

A CALL TO TRANSFORM THE INSTITUTION TO MEET THE NEEDS OF TODAY'S LEARNERS

Much of higher education was originally designed to meet the needs of 18- to 22-year-old full-time students who enter directly from high school. However, the New Majority of our students are older, likely to swirl among institutions, and have significant adult responsibilities outside of the classroom. The two companion books *Academic Transformation: A Design Approach for the New Majority* and *The New Majority Student: Working from Within to Transform Higher Education* are a call to transform colleges and universities to meet the academic and student experience needs of New Majority students and for adult educators to become advocates, allies, and resources for needed reforms.

Book contributors, including faculty, staff and administrators at public, private, and community colleges, provide insights for this transformation. Taking a personalized approach based on a wide range of experiences, the contributors provide a framework for cross-campus conversations and collaborations to help stakeholders across the institution to understand New Majority learners' strengths, needs, and challenges within an increasingly competitive educational market.

Academic Transformation: A Design Approach for the New Majority begins with a description of New Majority learners, explores enrollment management and student experience considerations, articulates a retention model and adapted high impact practices to support student success, navigates technology considerations, and addresses the impact of academic transformation for New Majority learners on higher-education finance.

The New Majority Student: Working from Within to Transform Higher Education utilizes a business perspective to academic transformation, providing a guide to how universities can redefine and restructure their education product to meet student needs. Taking a human-centered design approach, the contributors provide frameworks and examples of how institutions can reallocate technology, effort (internal, external, student, faculty) and finances to re-imagine programs and ensure long-term institutional health.

ONE

An Introduction to the New Majority

Eric Malm

This is a book about the need for higher education institutions to change to meet the needs of a changing student population. Increasingly our classrooms include students who are older, may work full or part time, and may have significant family responsibilities. For these students, school competes with many other life demands. We refer to these students as the "New Majority" and estimate this growing group now represents more than 68 percent of all undergraduates nationwide.[1]

We believe that by raising awareness of the nature and needs of this New Majority of learners, we will provide a valuable contribution to the universities, teachers, and student–learners. The chapters in this book highlight ways of thinking about how to meet the learning needs of New Majority students and suggest areas across the academic enterprise that could be refashioned or modified to better help serve these students. Although change is never easy, we believe that with effort and commitment, institutions can transform themselves to better serve New Majority students.

WHO IS THE NEW MAJORITY?

Within the university and the culture of the admissions office, *traditional* students are those who are eighteen, starting college immediately after high school graduation, and are first-time, full-time students typically enrolled in fifteen to eighteen credit hours per semester. More often than not, they are residential students who are engaged in campus activities and probably have a part-time job on or off campus. These students will want to remain on track to graduate in four years, and we know they are eager to move on to their careers.

As faculty, when we think of students, we think of first-time, full-time students who are mainly interested in being good students and having fun while they are in school. For those of us who are teachers, we expect *our* class to be their top priority. If these students stick to their knitting, we expect them to graduate in four years (or three and a half, if they're really motivated) and then move out into the adult world after graduation. We assume that the vast majority of our students fit into this category.

The second admissions term of interest to us is the *nontraditional student*, but even these are somewhat traditional, too, in that we use this term to describe adult returning students, students who are older than age twenty-two, may be veterans, part-time students, parents, and commuters. We have special academic units for adult learners and adult students, continuing education offices, and night and weekend classes to "accommodate" them as students. We also know that there are nontraditional students in our classrooms, but at most institutions the attention is squarely on the traditional undergraduate student. We have designed our entire institution—from recruiting and enrollment, residence life, financial aid, academic support, career services—around the eighteen to twenty-two year-old who has come to us directly from high school.

We need to move beyond the terms *traditional* and *nontraditional* because campus demographics, along with students' expectations for the value and benefits of higher education, have changed. As costs have increased, so have the financial pressures that students face. Today about 40 percent of full-time undergraduates age twenty-four or younger worked, and more than 75 percent of part-time students age twenty-four or younger worked.[2] A recent study suggests that 82 percent of undergraduates couldn't afford to go to school without working.[3] And time spent working isn't the only challenge students face, as we'll see later in the chapter.

In this book, we define a new category, the *New Majority* (illustrated in Figure 1.1), to help focus attention on the fact that our student population has changed in significant ways. We posit the New Majority as consisting of two different groups—working adults age twenty-five or older pursuing an undergraduate degree and students ages eighteen to twenty-four who are going to school *and* have significant adult responsibilities. Although there are many ways of viewing and quantifying adult responsibilities, in Figure 1.1 we break them down into financial independence and "other" adult responsibilities (such as having dependents).

New Majority now represents the plurality of total undergraduate students today and will continue to grow in number. But this significant change has not yet been fully realized or absorbed by stakeholders in higher education. The purpose of this book is to better describe the New

An Introduction to the New Majority

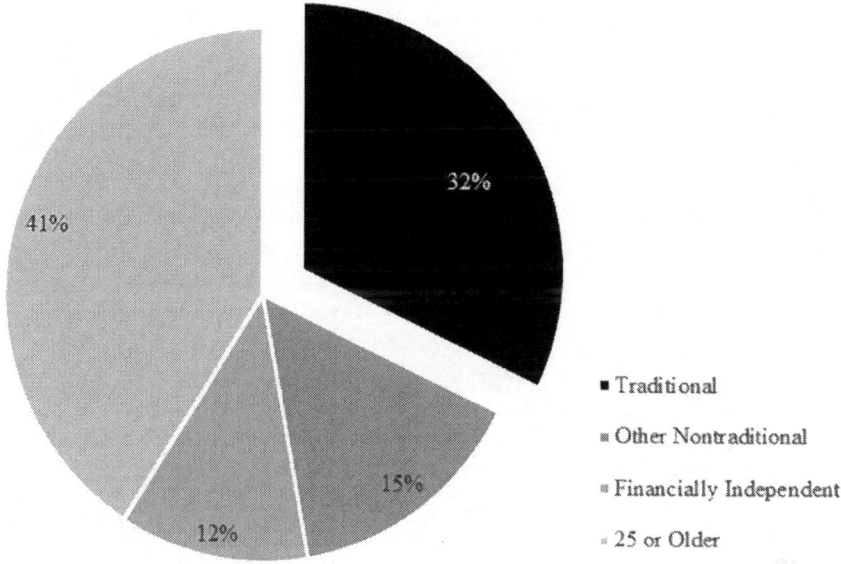

Figure 1.1. The New Majority: Traditionally aged, financially dependent students are now the minority. Source: Author's calculations using NCES Power-Stat 2012 data, NCES Enrollment Data, and ICES Web Tables.

Majority and describe a broad set of changes that can help institutions provide better, more accessible, and affordable learning experiences, and to provide a context for institution-wide conversations about change.

REALLY? ... IN MY CLASS?

It's a surprise to many that the New Majority is, in fact, the majority of undergraduates today. Let's first examine the expanding pool of adult learners. According to the National Center for Education Statistics, in 2013 there were about 8.1 million undergraduate students age twenty-five or older, representing more than 40 percent of the approximately 20 million undergraduate students enrolled that year.[4]

But what exactly do we mean by *traditionally aged students with adult responsibilities*, and how do these responsibilities differ from those of the past? The growing importance and impact of these adult responsibilities has been studied for several years. For example, a US Department of Education 2002 study by Susan Choy is widely cited and attempted to define and quantify the term *nontraditional*.[5] Table 1.1 shows the percentage of students who fell into each of six categories that marked a student as nontraditional.

As you'll see, although the percentages vary significantly by institution type, they are significant (and perhaps surprising). This data starts to paint a picture of a student population that may be "hiding" among our traditionally aged students—students who have significant financial and family responsibilities.

So how many traditional students do we have left? Although the numbers depend on how attributes such as financial independence are defined, a report from the American Council on Education (ACE) suggests that as few as 15 percent of undergraduates still fit in the traditional label.[6] Research by the Center for Postsecondary and Economic Success finds that about half of students are "independent," about a quarter are parents, about 15 percent are single parents, more than a quarter are employed full-time, and nearly 4 in 10 employed part-time.[7] Between 2005 and 2015, the cost of tuition room and board increased by 33 percent at public institutions and 26 percent at private institutions, after adjusting for inflation.[8] The point is that with today's high tuition costs, fewer and fewer students can afford the luxury of attending college full-time without working.

Anecdotally, professors will tell you students are changing. When students don't seem to be as focused or engaged as we would hope, what's a teacher to do? We could complain that students aren't responsible or don't take their studies seriously. We could complain about the admissions department or about an ineffective K–12 system. Or we could learn to change to better serve these student–customers.

Whether one takes the business view that students are our customers, and we need to produce a product that works for them, or whether we view it as the job of higher education to produce well-informed citizens

Table 1.1. Percentage of undergraduates with nontraditional characteristics, by type of institution

Type of institution	Financially independent	Attended part-time	Delayed enrollment	Worked full-time	Had dependents	Single parent
Total	50.9	47.9	45.5	39.3	26.9	13.3
Public two-year	63.7	69.5	58.7	53.8	34.5	16.4
Public four-year	37.6	33.3	31.5	25.5	17.6	9.2
Private nonprofit four-year	36.7	27.6	34.0	28.5	18.8	8.6
Private for-profit	72.9	21.5	67.8	40.8	44.3	26.6

who possess critical-thinking and information-literacy skills necessary to contribute to society, it's becoming clear that institutions need to find more effective ways of serving our students.

EVIDENCE OF A PROBLEM

Although there are clearly many factors that contribute to low completion rates, the factors that today's adult and independent students face make completion increasingly difficult. Studies of non-completion show financial and employment issues as being the main reasons students stopped their education before completing their degree.[9] There is a clear similarity in the reasons for non-completion cited in Figure 1.2 and the attributes of the nontraditional student. Family and financial issues can be difficult to balance in our traditional setting.

Low degree-completion rates are one sign that many students are not being adequately served. Nationally, 58 percent of students who enter a full-time four-year program graduate within six years. Students entering less selective colleges with open enrollment complete degrees just 34 percent of the time within six years and 27 percent at for-profit institutions.[10]

Although there are certainly many factors that impact degree completion, when students start college but walk away without a degree, institutions should be concerned. And lack of completion today means an in-

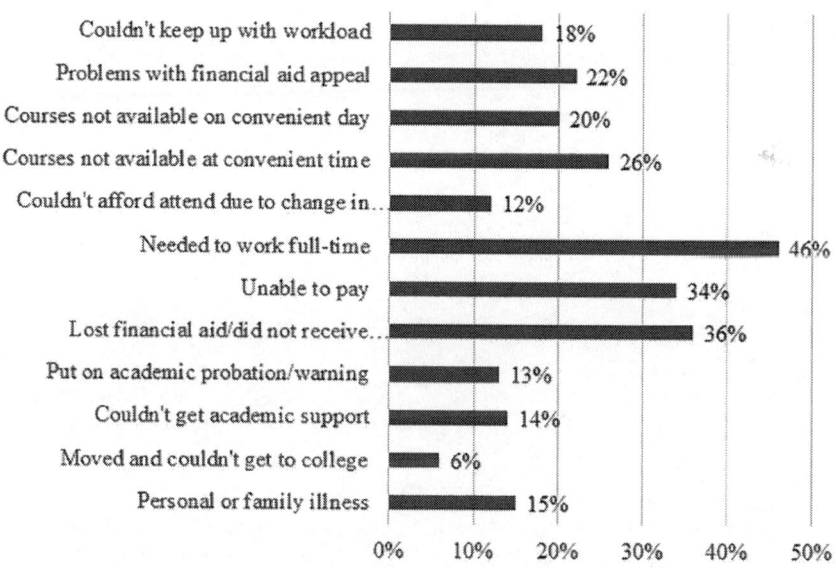

Figure 1.2. Reasons for non-completion. Source: Sonia Ninon. (2013). *Non-Returning Students Survey Results.* Indianapolis, IN: Ivy Technical College.

creasing population of adults who are likely to return in the future, perhaps discouraged and in debt. With around 31 million students who started college in the past twenty years but did not earn a degree,[11] it's clear that the ranks of the New Majority will continue to increase.

Student-debt burdens are another sign of a problem. In 2016, the average debt of graduating students was $25,902 for public four-year institutions and $29,657 for private four-year institutions with 60 percent and 64 percent of students, respectively, graduating with debt. And debt without a degree is even a tougher problem. An analysis by Education Policy found that in 2009, 54 percent of students in for-profit institutions dropped out, an increase of 20 percentage points from 2001.[12] So although many adult students are choosing for-profit institutions and community colleges, completion rates are low, and the percentage of students graduating with debt but no degree is too high.

The pressures faced by the learners with adult responsibilities, such as work and family commitments, also reveal themselves in the enrollment choices students are making. Figure 1.3 shows undergraduate enrollment by student age and institution type. Although the for-profit sector is still small in absolute numbers, a large percentage of their student–customers are adult learners. We see that the more agile for-profit institutions are disproportionately attracting older students who are attracted by flexibly structured classes.

As students have searched for convenience and affordability, enrollment in online courses has increased. Figure 1.4 shows the number of students taking at least one online course from 2002 to 2012, growing from 9.6 percent to 33.5 percent of students. The growth and change in the course formats that students choose to take also reinforces the idea that these students face a variety of completing needs, and more flexibly formatted online and hybrid courses may meet their needs. These choices may be driven more by cost and convenience and may not actually provide the highest levels of learning. Administrators are concerned with low course-completion rates for online courses,[13] so the migration to online programs should be viewed with caution.

HOW ARE NEW MAJORITY LEARNERS DIFFERENT?

It's not just the lifestyles and challenges that make New Majority learners different. Mind-set is also important. Although some traditional undergraduates may consider themselves *students who work*, New Majority students may view themselves as *employees who study*.[14] This distinction illustrates student mind-set. Do students view themselves first as students or as workers? The distinction has impacts in the classroom. Students who view themselves as workers first may lack confidence in themselves as students. Professors who can leverage the knowledge and experience

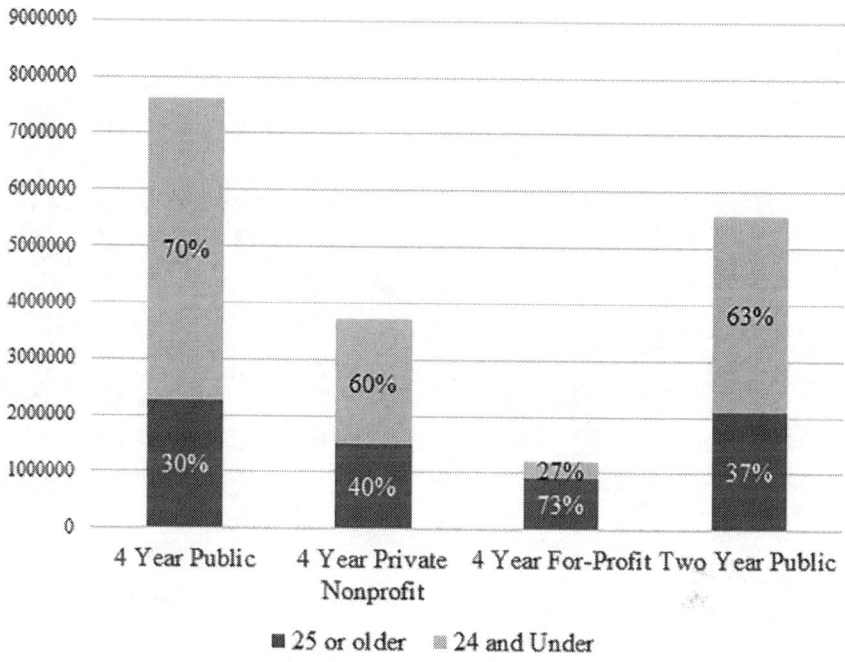

Figure 1.3. Undergraduate enrollment by student age and institution type.
Source: National Student Clearinghouse Research Center (2016).

from the work world are likely to help these employees who work to achieve more. But this requires both a realization on the part of faculty, as well as a shift in teaching and assignment styles.

Adults who have started but not completed college have been the focus of numerous foundation and government studies. Researchers understand important ways in which adult learners are different, and many of the types of practices that can more effectively help these students succeed.

A report by Erisman and Steel (2015) on Lumina Foundation adult degree-completion efforts asserts "the problem is that this knowledge about the differences between traditional college students and adult learners has not been factored into the pedagogy and operations of nearly enough colleges and universities . . . , adults returning to college to complete a degree need a higher education system that is more affordable, flexible and student-centered than the one that currently exists."[15]

Erisman and Steel's analysis points to several broad categories of need. Adult students need particular kinds of outreach and recruitment efforts. Adults who are near completion are surprisingly difficult to reach to make the case to return to studies, but strides have been made to

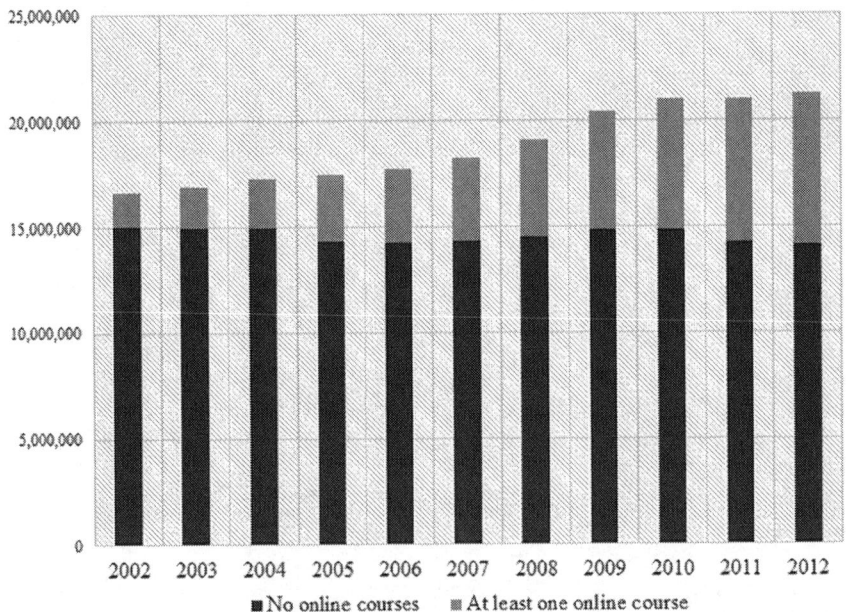

Figure 1.4. Students taking at least one online course. Source: National Student Clearinghouse Research Center (2016).

communicate with these students more effectively. Once "in the pipeline," student support services are critical.

Issues like determining credit transfer and credit for prior learning are important, as are conversations about financial and academic support. Academic programs need to be structured with a focus on how degree completion can be linked to career success. At the course level, flexibility is important, as is the ability to leverage student strengths to boost confidence and accelerate completion. Technology plays an important role in making the whole experience more accessible and dynamic.

THE ROAD AHEAD

The chapters in this book help identify specific strategies that can be used to help reshape how our colleges and universities operate. The chapter contributors include faculty, staff, and administrators from public, private, and community colleges. The viewpoints, experience, and active participation of multiple stakeholders is necessary for institutional change to be successful. Written from their particular stakeholder perspectives, each chapter author describes key issues relating to meeting the needs of New Majority students.

We have intentionally written this book in a conversational voice. It is important that conversations take place across campuses, within and between stakeholder groups. Although we hope that (for example) instructional designers will gain some benefit from reading the chapter written by the instructional designer, we feel it's even more important for people who are *not* instructional designers to read the chapter. As you read, we hope that you feel like you are part of a broader conversation. And we hope that you'll continue this conversation with a host of stakeholders on your campus.

In chapter 2, Ayisha Sereni describes "The Pragmatic Mind-Set of New Majority Students." Speaking from her perspectives as an adult student, a faculty member, and an administrator at a community college, Sereni understands both the challenges and strengths that adult learners bring to the table. The reader gains a deeper understanding of the various paths that adult learners have taken in and out of higher education. Sereni pays special attention to emotional intelligence and draws attention to some of the skills and attributes that have allowed adult learners to succeed without a college degree. Adaptability, intrinsic motivation, and emotional intelligence are central themes. She describes various ways in which programs can be designed to leverage these assets at both the faculty and institutional levels.

In "Providing Student-Centered Support for Adult Students," Patricia Griffin, executive director for the Center for Adult Education and Lifelong Learning at Cabrini University, argues that a student-centered support infrastructure is critical for the success of adult learners. She draws on decades of experience as both a teacher and administrator in describing specific considerations for how support services should be designed for of New Majority learners.

Marguerite Weber describes how adapted high-impact practices can be used to help better engage adult learners in "Fit/Fear/Focus: Developing Learners' Sense of Belonging, Security, and Hope." An expert on course redesign and adult education, Weber describes her Fit-Fear-Focus model for retention and institutional effectiveness and shows how the model can translate into a set of adapted high-impact practices to meet the needs and challenges of working adult students. A central theme of this chapter is that these practices can be infused throughout an institution and used to help adult students succeed.

In "Technology: Higher Education Disruption and New Majority Learner Access," Paul Walsh, USMx project director, University System of Maryland, provides a longer-term view of how technology has disrupted "business as usual" in higher education. Throughout his academic career, Walsh has bridged the gap between the academic and IT "sides of the house." Walsh speaks critically about how institutions, including faculty, need to actively embrace technology and explore its various roles for improving learning. As he says, just as "a dentist who didn't keep up on the latest technology to fight cavities would quickly lose business," faculty, staff, and administrators need to continually consider how technology can transform and improve our product.

Bill Egan, instructional designer for the Penn State World Campus, shares his experiences working with faculty to design courses that use technology to redefine the classroom and meet the needs of returning adult students. In "Program and Course Design for the New Majority," Egan draws on his experience developing online, hybrid, and distance courses at a large state university. Egan stresses the importance of designing entire programs with input from stakeholders across the institution, including teachers, enrollment and marketing staff, and administrators. Program-level considerations and funding for proper course development are critical before course-level change can proceed.

Marguerite Weber joins me in a chapter "The Financial Dimension: Institutional Readiness for New Majority Learners." Money matters, for both students and the institution. We have just seen that financial challenges are a major reason cited by adult learners for noncompletion, so developing affordable ways to package and present programs is crucial to attracting and retaining adult students. This chapter also addresses the tensions that exist between operating costs and student-learning outcomes. These considerations are particularly important when designing programs that restructure time and roles and use technology in newer ways. A central theme of this chapter is that academic redesign efforts need to reallocate not just time and effort but financial resources as well. Proper funding of shared resources is particularly important; funding shifts must mirror changes in how classes and programs are structured and delivered.

The final chapter on "Learning with Others: Working with Others to Build the New Majority Institution" describes the leadership challenges that are faced when implementing change across an entire academic organization. Beverly Schneller, associate provost for academic affairs at Belmont University, with decades of experience with accreditation, joins Weber and Malm to provide insight on ways to engage stakeholders in the change process. Malm describes challenges from the perspective of the chair of a faculty technology committee; Weber draws on her teaching experience and work as vice president of adult programs and more recently as vice president of student affairs, and Schneller examines how the ideas presented in this volume may be used to transform, innovate, and engage higher education leadership in important conversations about students, student-learning outcomes, and understanding both institutional and student success.

A central theme of the final chapter is the importance of innovative cross-unit collaborations and open dialog between all stakeholders on campus who can contribute to building a dynamic learning environment for New Majority institutions. Keys to the success of any institutional transformation efforts are being attentive to varied levels of transparency, awareness of student goals for college completion, and building a climate of trust that fosters sustainability once innovations are in place.

NOTES

1. Author's calculations using the following data. The percentage of financially independent students was calculated for students for ages twenty-five and older and twenty-four or younger using the National Center for Education Statistics PowerStat tool using 2012 data. The number of students by age came from the NCES Enrollment Data Table 303.40, using 2012. The percentage of "other nontraditional" students twenty-four or younger are the author's estimate.
2. National Center for Education Statistics (2015), *College Student Employment*. Retrieved from http://nces.ed.gov/programs/coe/indicator_ssa.asp
3. P. Attewell and; D. Lavin (2012), "The other 75%: College education beyond the elite," in E. C. Langemann & H. Lewis (Eds.), *What Is College for? The Public Purpose of Higher Education* (New York: Teachers College, Columbia University).
4. National Center for Educational Statistics (2016), *Characteristics of Postsecondary Students*. Retrieved July 10, 2017, from https://nces.ed.gov/programs/coe/indicator_csb.asp
5. Susan Choy (2001), *Nontraditional Undergraduates*. Retrieved July 10, 2017, from http://nces.ed.gov/pubs2002/2002012.pdf
6. Louise Soares (2013), *Post-traditional Learners and the Transformation of Postsecondary Education: A Manifesto for College Leaders*. American Council on Education. Retrieved July 10, 2017, from: http://www.acenet.edu/news-room/Documents/Post-traditional-Learners.pdf
7. Center for Postsecondary and Economic Success (2015), *Yesterday's Non-Traditional Student Is Today's Traditional Student*. Retrieved July 10, 2017, from http://www.clasp.org/resources-and-publications/publication-1/CPES-Nontraditional-students-pdf.pdf
8. National Center for Education Statistics (2016), *Fast Facts: Tuition Costs of Colleges and Universities*. Retrieved July 11, 2017, from https://nces.ed.gov/fastfacts/display.asp?id=76
9. Sonia Ninon (2013), *Non-Returning Students Survey Results* (Indianapolis, IN: Ivy Technical College). Retrieved July 10, 2017, from https://www.ivytech.edu/files/IR__13161_Non-Returning_Student_Survey_Results_Final.pdf
10. National Center for Education Statistics (2016), "Fast Facts: Graduation Rates." Retrieved July 11, 2017, from https://nces.ed.gov/fastfacts/display.asp?id=40
11. National Student Clearinghouse Research Center (2014), *Some College, No Degree: A National View of Students with Some College Enrollment, But No Completion*. Retrieved from July 10, 2017, from https://nscresearchcenter.org/signaturereport7/
12. Education Policy Center (2012), *Degreeless in Debt: What Happens to Borrowers Who Drop Out*. Retrieved July 10, 2017, from http://educationpolicy.air.org/publications/degreeless-debt-what-happens-borrowers-who-drop-out
13. Elaine Allen and Jeff Seaman (2014), *Grade Change: Tracking Online Education in the United States*. Retrieved July 10, 2017, from http://www.onlinelearningsurvey.com/reports/gradechange.pdf
14. Soares, *Post-traditional Learners and the Transformation of Postsecondary Education*.
15. Wendy Erisman and Patricia Steele (2015), *Adult College Completion in the 21st Century: What We Know and What We Don't*. Retrieved July 11, 2017, from https://higheredinsight.files.wordpress.com/2015/06/adult_college_completion_20151.pdf

TWO

The Pragmatic Mind-Set of New Majority Students

Ayisha Sereni

New Majority students are pragmatic about the costs and time needed to attain a degree or credential and weigh that investment against competition for their attention in the form of jobs, family, and other personal commitments.

Today, most students are balancing school with a significant number of work hours to meet college expenses; however, one characteristic of many New Majority learners is that they are balancing more than school and work. They have extensive commitments to family, community, and the workplace.

According to 2012 National Postsecondary Student Aid Study data, "[Nontraditional] students carry the responsibilities of advancing their academic goals while balancing the demands of parenthood. In the 2011–2012 academic year, 29% of public community college students indicated that they were parents. Of those students, 53% were single parents. These were much higher rates than students at public four-year institutions, where only 12% of the students reported they had children—42% of whom were single parents."[1]

In many instances, New Majority learners serve as primary caretaker for both children, and aging parents. In these situations, a person is referred to as being a part of the "sandwich generation," inserted in the middle of two generations that require care should the need arise.[2]

Because of these concerns, New Majority learners' commitment to persisting at an institution depends on access and affordability issues more than any other factor. Therefore, they tend to fall into one of three categories:

1. They attended college but had negotiated matriculation with scant access to information concerning college choices and options.
2. They wanted to attend college but had to delay entry because of circumstances beyond their control.
3. They attended college and left before earning a credential or degree and are subsequently returning to complete what they started.

For the first category, New Majority learners may be invisible to their college institutions. Fresh out of high school and into the classroom, they may feel a step behind others who had college-completing family members and other forms of advanced preparation. The second and third groups likely are comprised of older students with work and other adult experiences, and they too feel a bit behind the imagined "traditional" students in the class, whom they perceive as having had more advantages, more preparation, and more support.

My college story fits this framework, first as a student, second as a faculty member, and third as a community college dean. As did I, New Majority students will decide to engage in higher education under two conditions: they conclude that a college credential equates to economic security, and they recognize that personal circumstances are manageable to the point that academic pursuits are possible.

Now, through the leveraging of technology and the application of innovative scheduling models, students with backgrounds that decades ago were underrepresented in college have found that earning a college credential and keeping up with competing priorities is no longer a dream. In fact, this new wave of nontraditional students has earned its own name and are referred to as the *New Majority* because they comprise 68 percent of all undergraduate college students, thus outweighing the traditional college student paradigm that has dominated the higher education market for decades.

PERSONAL PERSPECTIVES

Student Perspective

As a child of immigrants from the former Yugoslavia, I was the first in my family to attend college. When I was two years old, my father became terminally ill with bone cancer likely acquired from working in the steel plants; when he passed away, I became the four-year-old child of a single parent who was determined her child would go to college and who reinforced that an education would be the key to success.

As with many immigrant parents, Mom did not know to encourage advanced-placement courses or to engage in activities that would look good on a college application. With emotional and often limited financial support, and even more limited understanding of college-going, first-generation students can experience a sense of being unprepared for college in ways not connected with the strength of their academic skills. After high school, first-generation students may be college bound but unprepared academically, financially, or mentally to go to college. Importantly, this lack of preparation includes missing tools to assess college-going options to find a good fit for still unformed goals. Decision processes thus focus on expedience and cost.

Fortunately, there was a community college nearby, so I earned an associate's degree in general studies. After completing the associate degree, it would take transferring twice before completing the baccalaureate.

Throughout my undergraduate career, likely no one at my college, including me, would have identified my experience as "nontraditional"—and certainly not "New Majority"—as the experience was still a minority experience. Many high school classmates whose parents had not attended college had gone to work full-time and had delayed or skipped going to college all together. However, the feeling of being out of step, unprepared, and unaware made the college experience different from that of most college classmates. The lack of understanding of what it would take to be successful in college, coupled with the lack of specific support to address gaps in understanding, likely extended time to graduation and created occasions of risks to stop out, drop out, or flounder.

When it was time to start graduate coursework, the struggle proved too much, and after completing only one semester, I quit the program and instead pursued an industry credential that was more immediately work relevant. It was a practical decision to increase work value and income rather than achieve more personal goals.

Fifteen years later, finally returning to pursue those goals, the outward look of a traditional learner was gone. A fully online program was the only way to return to studies to prepare to teach at the college level. Therefore, returning to higher education after a fifteen-year absence was possible because it met the conditions described: completing an (additional) college credential connected to economic security and personal circumstances and academic demands could be managed because the program was fully online.

The grueling schedule was a hallmark of the New Majority experience: two years of balancing full-time work, caring for the family of a husband and two young boys, and completing coursework to earn the master's degree, followed by six more years of the same to earn a doctoral degree, again through an online program. My immediate exigencies and my future goals constrained program options. This was the only path for completion for me, although often students in fully online programs can experience a sense of being disconnected with other learners or have a sense of longing for a campus experience where they can personally connect to resources and informal learning opportunities.

Dean Perspective

Now those experiences as a first-generation student, a nontraditional transfer student, and an adult in online graduate programs inform my work as a community college dean. From this vantage point, the students I directly encounter are on opposite ends of the student-success continuum. Either they are receiving awards at celebrations of their achievements, or they are coming to my attention because they are experiencing academic or personal problems that are interfering with their pursuit of a credential. At a recent event to celebrate students in the early stages of their academic journeys, one student came in with four of her children in tow, ages newborn to middle school. She had given birth to the youngest child in the middle of the semester and returned to class just days after giving birth!

In other instances, New Majority students come to see the dean when they have encountered a problem in the classroom. Although some clashes relate to misbehavior and bad choices, other barriers to success range from instructors who are not willing to adjust practices or policies to support the unusual circumstance(s) that a New Majority student may face such as needing access to a cell phone during class for emergency calls to complaints related to lack of flexibility with policies or procedures.

As dean, and especially as one who identifies with the perspective of a New Majority learner, personal focus is on providing faculty with information related to the New Majority population that helps to raise awareness. In addition, when interviewing new instructors, candidates are asked questions concerning the strengths and needs of New Majority students. The first check is for awareness of this population and their respective needs.

Prospective faculty members must demonstrate specific strategies to effectively "serve" this type of student. The successful candidates show understanding that the success of New Majority students is essential to the institution's success. The better we show agility with flexible assignments, building on students' mature work and life experiences, and articulating the pragmatic value of the learning at hand, the better we serve all students.

To engage current faculty and staff, student testimonials provide needed perspective. Best practices include student panel presentations on issues related to access, affordability, and support services that matter; other ways to make New Majority learners visible in the institution is to incorporate student speakers at staff retreats and even to create video clips that highlight students' stories of the strengths of their commitment, resolve, and resilience and the returns on investments to individualize learning and services. Their presence unites faculty, students, and staff in a common experience of modern life; it is complicated, relational, and multilayered.

Faculty Perspective

As with many working in higher education today, the intricacy of New Majority learning remains. Thus, highly developed skills in technology and personal management are needed to meet complex responsibilities at work, in personal life, and in serving the community. In online classes, more and more students, in fact most of them, are also maintaining this difficult balance and succeed by virtue of their tremendous resilience, persistence, and drive.

In instances when a student is not doing well, it is commonly due to lack of familiarity with current technologies that support their learning. A New Majority learner may take longer to adapt to a new technology or have an outright aversion to technology altogether. Often, New Majority learners report that the last time they conducted academic research required digging through a card catalog. Today, students conduct research using a computer and the Internet. As a faculty member, it is important to maintain an awareness of these types of potential barriers and to establish an approach that fosters student success while maintaining academic integrity.

Others are unfamiliar with using computer tools to organize or develop their writing and instead focus on using text tools only to create the final "typed" product. Still others prefer paper-based reading tasks over online, multimedia learning resources because they can apply the outlining and underlining skills that worked for them in prior learning environments and in their workplaces, and they can also bring the book and notebook with them to use during work breaks or while transporting children to activities.

Still other conflicts are a result of pressing and recurring circumstances that cause the student to need to prioritize family or work obligations over personal academic pursuits. Faculty should also remember that New Majority learners are making personal, professional, and family sacrifices to honor their academic obligations as well. The promise of earning a college credential and attaining the associated benefits gives them an urgency to continually calculate risks and rewards and gains and losses, and we need to respect that enormous effort and good will.

New Majority learners can and do have a positive impact on "traditional" peers. Their life experiences offer a valuable perspective to traditional students. In teaching a class enrolled by both New Majority and more traditional learners, a good practice is to pair them up. Initially, faculty report resistance, with students expressing a wish to be paired with someone "more like me." They wonder, "What do I have in common with this person?" A recent assignment for a small business development and management class involved students assuming the role of investor in evaluating business ideas on the GoFundMe website. Students with limited professional experience benefited from the questions and comments of New Majority learners because their experiences provided insight that otherwise would not have been available.

In my college's real estate prelicensing classes, the advantage of experience usually presents as New Majority students having bought, sold, or rented a home, whereas traditional students may still live at home and therefore have minimal if any insight on these experiences.

New Majority students have a high level of pride, integrity, and accountability. As a faculty member, it is vital to be aware of these traits and to foster an environment that allows a New Majority learner to thrive. This can be accomplished by treating New Majority learners as the responsible adults they are and being prepared to adapt to the unique learning needs or circumstances that arise.

ATTRIBUTES FOR NEW MAJORITY LEARNER SUCCESS

Regardless of which combination of responsibilities the New Majority learner is harmonizing, New Majority learners must draw on some common attributes to persist and succeed in earning a college degree. These include adaptability, self-determination or intrinsic motivation, and emotional intelligence.

Adaptability

Introducing the goal of earning a college credential to an already-full plate adds a substantial commitment and burden on the New Majority learner who is already at capacity. Salovey and Mayer suggest that success is dependent on a student's ability to adapt to the demands of a given situation.[3] A high level of adaptability is essential to the success of the New Majority learner. Whether dealing with sick child, a deadline at work, or having to apply a novel skill in class, being fluid and nimble provides a New Majority learner the means to navigate unchartered waters with certainty.

College faculty and administration can foster an adaptive environment by creating policies and practices that consider unexpected situations that may arise and are out of the control of a New Majority learner. Naturally, it is critical to balance this flexibility with academic integrity. I have seen students leverage incomplete grades to finish coursework after the semester has ended. Some institutions allow students to transfer tuition to another section of the same course that may start later in the semester, eliminating the fear of a withdrawal on a transcript, which has financial aid implications, or the loss of tuition monies from employer support or from personal funding.

Intrinsic Motivation

One may ask what drives one New Majority learner to successfully manage multiple responsibilities, while another New Majority learner may barely make do or may find the struggle too much to sustain. For many, the answer comes down to intrinsic motivation, defined broadly as a person's enthusiasm and willingness to complete a task or to work assiduously toward reaching a goal. This drive is a force that guides and steers a person through adversity and through sacrifices needed to reach the finish line.

A prominent theoretical approach to intrinsic motivation is self-determination theory (SDT), which suggests that intrinsic motivation is fueled by direction, persistence, and intensity of the motivated behavior. Therefore, the New Majority learner who finds earning a college credential more intrinsically motivating will invest a strong degree of intensity in activities related to the accomplishment of the attainment of a college credential.[4]

A faculty member or administrator can turn to Maslow's Hierarchy of Needs theory to cultivate and sustain the intrinsic motivation that a New Majority learner holds. Specifically, cultivating feelings of accomplishment and prestige whenever possible, along with assisting New Majority learners with achieving their full potential, will serve to support the intrinsic motivation that is already there.

Emotional Intelligence

In addition to self-determination and being intrinsically motivated, a successful New Majority learner will likely need to possess emotional intelligence. Emotional intelligence, which merges emotions and intelligence, is defined as a group of cognitive activities that helps people recognize their feelings and those of others.[5] Emotional intelligence is a component of human intelligence that influences one's ability to identify, comprehend, control, and use emotions in solving problems of a personal and interpersonal nature.[6,7]

A New Majority student who is applying emotional intelligence in day-to-day activities possesses a keen ability to clearly recognize emotions personally and in others, to leverage emotion to support thoughts and actions, to recognize how emotions impact personal actions and those of others, and to regulate emotional responses.[8] New Majority students who recognize emotions in themselves and in others can assist with successfully balancing team projects with other classmates, can deal with faculty or coursework perceived as "challenging," and can better maintain family responsibilities that arise unexpectedly.

Emotions may assist with rational decision making resulting in stable behaviors.[9] A New Majority learner will apply this skill to navigate the daily pressures of managing multiple responsibilities in a sometimes-ambiguous environment. Relatedly, intelligence involves abstract capabilities such as identifying parallels between unrelated matters as well as evaluating individual components to recognize their likeness individually and collectively. Thus, when balancing multiple responsibilities, a New Majority learner can ultimately align efforts and sacrifices to the possibilities of what life can be like by earning a college credential. This abstract thinking requires the processing of one's thoughts.[10]

SUGGESTIONS FOR THE HIGHER EDUCATION SECTOR

Knowing that New Majority learners possess a high level of adaptability, self-determination or intrinsic motivation, and emotional intelligence, there are several suggestions for those working in the higher education sector.

First, *raise awareness* of the New Majority learner and implement practices that support the unique learning needs of this population. Examples include offering faculty development workshops that provide insight as to what New Majority students might bring to a classroom and how the faculty member can help support this student while maintaining the integrity of the coursework. As mentioned previously in this chapter, this can be accomplished by hosting student panel presentations, inviting students to speak at staff retreats as well as creating video clips that highlight students' stories.

Second, with the understanding that although New Majority learners are likely highly motivated students who have an intrinsic drive to earn a college credential, *help them keep the momentum along the way* by offering kudos, acknowledgments, and targeted support. Advising management and student success tracking tools such as Starfish can facilitate sending progress notes that simply communicate notice of how hard a student is working and encouragement to keep up the great work. If a tool such as Starfish is not available, sending an e-mail or even taking a moment to pull a student aside goes a long way.

Next, by *leveraging technology*, the needs of New Majority learners can be met. For example, exploring alternative teaching modalities can support students whose circumstances might otherwise make it impossible to come to campus because they can instead tune in from a mobile device or home computer. Conversely, the use of technology brings with it a skill set that New Majority learners may need assistance with developing. With any technology that is introduced, it is important to include a well-planned training opportunity along with responsive technical support resources.

Additionally, offer programs in a manner that *considers the lifestyle needs* of New Majority learners. This may be a combination of accelerated courses, paired hybrid courses, and a full selection of offerings in winter sessions and summers. Students who can pursue part-time studies across the whole year can make a similar rate of progress as those who take full-time courses in only fall and spring, and the possibility of having a full-time graduation date at a part-time lifestyle is enormously popular and correlated with strong success rates.

Another option is to offer classes at times and in modalities that are flexible and adaptable to the already full schedule of a New Majority learner. Perhaps a totally online course is not feasible, nor is a class that is offered totally on campus. In this instance, apply instructional design techniques to meet the learning objectives of the course while meeting the needs of the New Majority learner.

A personal example of this is a class that met on a Saturday for eight hours, then students would complete work online and come together during a scheduled "synchronous" virtual session during the week for the classroom conversation. Many approaches include 100-percent online and accelerated courses; these provide conveniences, but much thought is needed to create a more customized or boutique-type offering that truly becomes a *service-oriented approach*.

In conclusion, the personal experiences related here show that New Majority learners are changing the face of higher education. Given the decline in the number of traditional-age students, the greater percentage of students who work a nontrivial number of hours while pursuing college credentials, and the ever-expanding ranges of credentialing choices that students face when exploring career goals, higher educational professionals must pay attention to serving New Majority learners.

Approaches to meeting their needs must be mainstreamed and shape our new way of doing things for all learners. Individualizing, accelerating, supporting, and continuously arguing the values proposition are forces that are part of the fabric of contemporary work, contemporary commerce, and even contemporary communication; therefore, these forces have become our students' expectations as they enter our world of work, commerce, and communication. Meeting and exceeding those expectations is crucial to our own success.

NOTES

1. National Center for Education Statistics (n.d.), *National Postsecondary Student Aid Study—Overview*. Retrieved April 25, 2017, from https://nces.ed.gov/surveys/npsas/.

2. Ayala M. Pines, Margaret B. Neal, Leslie B. Hammer, and Tamar Icekson (2011), "Job Burnout and Couple Burnout in Dual-Earner Couples in the Sandwiched Generation." *Social Psychology Quarterly* 74, no. 4: 361–386. doi:10.1177/0190272511422452.

3. Peter Salovey, and John D. Mayer (1990), "Emotional intelligence." *Imagination, Cognition and Personality* 9, no. 3: 185–211.

4. Ruth Kanfer, Gilad Chen, and Robert D. Pritchard, eds. (2012), *Work Motivation: Past, Present and Future* (New York: Routledge).

5. Karin Klenke (2002), "Cinderella stories of women leaders: Connecting leadership contexts and competencies," *Journal of Leadership & Organizational Studies* 9, no. 2: 18–28.

6. Reuven Bar-On (2001), "Emotional intelligence and self-actualization," *Emotional Intelligence in Everyday Life: A Scientific Inquiry*: 82–97.

7. Salovey and Mayer, "Emotional intelligence."

8. Reuven Bar-On (1988), "The development of a concept of psychological well-being." Ph.D. dis., Rhodes University, South Africa; Daniel P. Goleman (1995), *Emotional Intelligence: Why It Can Matter More Than IQ for Character, Health and Lifelong Achievement* (New York: Bantam Books); John D. Mayer and Peter Salovey (1997), "What is emotional intelligence," in P. Salovey and D. Sluyter (Eds.), *Emotional Development and Emotional Intelligence: Educational Implications* (New York: Harper Collins), 3–34; David C. McClelland (1973), "Testing for competence rather than for intelligence," *American Psychologist* 28, no. 1: 1–14; and Salovey and Mayer, "Emotional intelligence."

9. David R. Caruso and Peter Salovey (2004), *The Emotionally Intelligent Manager: How to Develop and Use the Four Key Emotional Skills of Leadership* (Hoboken, NJ: John Wiley & Sons).

10. John D. Mayer, Peter Salovey, David R. Caruso, and Gill Sitarenios (2001), "Emotional intelligence as a standard intelligence," *Emotion* 1, no. 3: 232.

THREE

Providing Student-Centered Support for Adult Students

Patricia Griffin

BEING STUDENT CENTERED

Having a student-centered approach means reducing barriers to and creating opportunities for student success. Reflecting on specific strategies and efforts that have had immediate and sustainable impact, Bowl (2001) identifies three struggles that New Majority learners in higher education face: time poverty, financial poverty, and poverty of options and strategies to navigate institutional barriers.[1] The outlook of an experienced administrator focused primarily on adult students has repeatedly shown that adopting student-centered approaches is essential for the future of higher education. Being student-centered replaces the mind-set that organization and management are the focus with the perspective of seeking to understand the meaning these elements have for students.

COMING OUT OF THE SHADOWS

A transformative moment was during my service as secretary, then vice president, and eventually president of the Dean's and Directors of Adult Education (DACE) organization, which comprised deans and directors of adult and continuing education programs at Jesuit colleges and universities in the U.S. Colleagues at DACE are proud to "work at the margins" in our institutions and in the realm of higher education. Over many years leading adult programs at Saint Joseph's University, I had felt isolated from my colleagues and had developed a sense that the challenges were unique to this institution.

At DACE, there was a community of support and like-minded professionals who were focused primarily on the success of individual students, who just happened to be older than the usual student our institutions served. We shared laughter, tears of joy and frustration, and importantly, we discussed how to be fiscally responsible to our institutions, within our units, and for our students. We realized that "we" were on the cusp of disruptive innovation in our schools, often the gateway for introducing online learning. We also recognized that, with institution budget changes to responsibility-centered management strategies (RCM), if left unattended, our students and our areas could become obsolete.

Because the adult-serving programs represented at DACE largely had been designed to remain independent "schools" or "colleges" in their universities, they featured individualized processes and programs to support those now more accurately described as New Majority learners. Yet, with the advent of technology-mediated learning, institutions increasingly moved to standardize programs for these students, focusing on recruiting them to fill seats in online, hybrid, and accelerated courses without attention to a special student experience for adult learners.

Indeed, over the past five years, twelve of the twenty-eight universities represented in DACE no longer have a separate "Evening College" or "School of Professional or Continuing Education"; all students and programs are housed in the more traditional schools of business or arts & science. Although this movement of New Majority learners into the mainstream is the trend, unfortunately student support services have not always adjusted to meet the needs of the changing student population.

MEETING THE NEEDS OF ADULT LEARNERS

An example of access to coursework without attention to the student experience was part of my life as an adjunct teaching in the evening colleges at several Philadelphia area colleges. Classes ran from 6 PM to 10 PM, and students faced real physical barriers, including fighting with rush hour traffic that allowed no time for eating or decompressing after a day of work, lack of sufficient parking once arriving to campus, no access to food service or even vending machines, desks that were too small for adult bodies, having the registrar and financial aid offices closed at 5 PM, and little access to academic advisors, most of whom worked part-time and focused on course subsequent course enrollment.

Some schools did better than others. At one university, evening college students had several clubs, including student government, theater, chorus, and club sports. However, at two other schools, evening part-time students were not permitted to participate in extracurricular activities.

Having had experience with supporting adult learners out of the classroom, this perspective from inside the classroom was revelatory. First, the students' ability to focus on the course content was negatively impacted by lack of resources: they were hungry, they were uncomfortable in their seats, and they were stressed at not being able to pay their bills or register for their classes without losing hours at work or with their families. Second, the conditions posed a personal ethical conflict. The treatment was unjust, especially at predominantly faith-based private schools. It was a clear social justice issue.

This perspective has shaped my work while ascending to administrative positions of greater responsibility. The clear priorities have centered on first identifying and reducing out-of-the-class-room impediments to learners' abilities to focus and engage in a supportive student experience and then creating opportunities for the student and those who serve them to learn from one another and thus address the inherent injustice of a student experience that is not separate and not equal.

One endeavor ensures that the curriculum connects clearly to students' goals and life experiences. For example, program development should be based on local and regional employment data, so certifications and credentials have immediate use and long-term value. Planning and support work builds on close ties with alumni and advancement professionals, and through these collaborations, students have access to widened professional networks and funding streams for scholarships. Through true partnerships with student life offices, who themselves are struggling to meet the needs of more "invisible" New Majority learners, adult-focused student services can be shaped to more fully integrate all students into campus life.

Finally, and likely the most foundational, it's essential to establish relationships with auxiliary services including public safety, food service, and operations to address students' needs during "off times."

BECOMING MORE STUDENT CENTERED

Meeting the needs of New Majority student–customers takes the active work and participation from folks across campus. A student-centered institution should focus on the meaning of the learning opportunities for the student who is a good match for the strengths of the particular program; therefore, the actual processes, organization of time and space, operations and management will vary because of the characteristics of the student population. A few examples follow.

Admissions and Enrollment Management

Rolling admissions is extremely important for the New Majority. It is important to meet students in the context of where and when they are available. The cohort-based models that have gained acceptance for adult and continuing education programs may make sense for institutional planning, yet over time there must be sufficient flexibility for new students to enter and for continuing students to step out and then return, lest we contribute to the fallacy of managerialism as an effective strategy for increasing student enrollment and success in a highly competitive market.

In some institutions, there is a movement to centralize admissions and recruiting for all student levels into one unit area. Admissions counselors must be fully trained and competent to respond to questions surrounding academic programs, transfer credit, credit for prior learning, student-support services, and program outcomes as these relate to the New Majority student, as often these differ from the traditional undergraduate programs.

Coupled with these processes, a student-centered approach would facilitate ease of matriculation by providing a transfer-credit evaluation within 48 hours of application and would establish processes for a "warm hand-off" from admissions to the accepted student's academic advisor.

Along these lines, it is important that recruiting efforts look beyond the traditional transfer fair/community college locales. Engage with the New Majority in the spaces where they reside (i.e., collaborate with employers to hold information sessions, offer discounts or application fee waivers to community partners, and facilitate faculty experts for noncredit learning in the community to engage with adults); coffee shops, libraries, and community days are opportunities to engage with the New Majority.

Paper-based applications have been replaced by electronic applications. Importantly for the New Majority, these must be tailored to the adult applicant in content and delivery format. For example, in simple ways the application should avoid asking for unnecessary documents, such as a high school transcript, the high school GPA, or SAT scores when these are not required for admissions.

Program-to-Program Transfer Agreements with Community Colleges

In many four-year institutions of higher education, the academic offerings for the New Majority vary from those available to traditional transfer students. The college or university must aim to provide timely program-to-program guides for community college partners, their advisors, and potential adult transfer students. Many community colleges will post these online for prospective students to compare how their prior coursework and prior learning map to the four-year degree-completion program. This type of informal degree audit form and process increases opportunity for self-directed adult learners and their advisors to explore their options beyond the community college.

Shuttle Service to Area Public Transportation Hubs

One of the external barriers that the New Majority student may face is transportation to and from campus. One consideration may be access to public transportation, which includes late-evening and Saturday-route schedules. For the central city college, this may not pose a significant hindrance; however, for a student enrolled in college further outside the city, the proximity and schedules are more limited, and those institutions may consider shuttles or easy ride-sharing matching.

Because of carefully orchestrated commitments to work, family, and community, the New Majority student is highly sensitive to being on time. When a faculty member ends class "just a few moments late" or the shuttle driver doesn't adhere to a printed schedule, this could mean that the student must wait for an hour or longer until the next train or bus departs. New Majority students have described such situations as regular occurrences, resulting in their having to wait alone in the dark at a rail or bus station, and then not arriving home until close to midnight and then having to begin the commute to work at daybreak.

Academic Support

The New Majority student may face reentry challenges associated with writing, quantitative literacy, and subject content areas. Many schools are piloting online tutoring services supported with and through technology-enhanced video services. These are wonderful additions that provide scheduling flexibility for the adult learner and may similarly serve to reduce the burden on understaffed support areas.

Alumni Relations and Advancement Offices

The New Majority student is often a hidden source of strength for these key institutional areas. It is important that these units engage with the New Majority as early and as consistently as possible. Many of the students who make up the New Majority are employed, unlike the traditional undergraduate student. Though their contributions may be nominal at first, their emotional commitment to the college or university is strong on the front end. They have decided to invest their future in the college; as anyone in Advancement will tell you, the emotional commitment is a key driver to facilitate engagement.

The alumni network is frequently made up of those who completed their degree on a part-time basis or they know of someone who completed their degree in this nontraditional way. They understand the resilience and drive that it takes to succeed. Building on these characteristics is a positive way to develop mentoring and support networks for students in the New Majority. Lastly, these units are most often tasked with securing general and specific funding for campus projects. The New Majority student is frequently overlooked in setting these priorities; for a mission-driven liberal arts college, such an oversight may also be seen as an equity issue.

Other Service Areas, Including Food Service and Technology Support

In both these areas, resourcing for the New Majority has been a balancing act for institutions of higher education. Expanded course scheduling to include evenings, weekends, and online means that students expect to receive reasonable support during these hours. Although food service may require limited staffing associated with a kiosk or vending machines that carry a selection of healthy choices, there is increased demand for just-in-time technology support that extends 24/7/365 to support the New Majority student.

Orientation

Having an on-boarding process (orientation) for all levels of students is important, but one size does not fit all, and in fact, it may be more important for the part-time adult, graduate, and doctoral student than it is for the full-time traditional student. Like Wonacott, think about "Orientation as Retention."[2] When most adult students arrive on campus, the services are closed, food is scarce, and the campus may be dark and cold. Orientation provides a welcoming opportunity to be part of the campus community.

Components of a successful orientation for the New Majority require low investment of resources beyond staff time outside of the normal 9–5 workday hours. Making the orientation truly student centered, however, does require an investment of seeing the campus through the lens of an adult student.

For example, campus tours should highlight areas where to park in the evening, food service, the library and learning resource centers, and shuttle pick-up locations. They should not include a tour of the dorms! Ideally, these tours may be hosted by a current adult student or alum, but if this is not possible then the undergraduate student ambassadors must receive specialized training for areas and discussion points that will provide for a meaningful experience.

One other key component to orientation has been to offer a panel discussion, followed by questions and answers with current students and faculty. An effective orientation will seek to eliminate this frequently heard statement, "I wish that I had known that!"

At orientation, it is also valuable to have resource tables staffed by representatives from the Student Service Areas, including Financial Aid, the Registrar's Office, Health Services, and Academic Support Services, to greet and meet with attendees. This may be the only face-to-face opportunity for newly admitted students to interface with these areas, but having a name, a face, and business card provides clarity and reassurance for whom to contact as students make steady progress to degree completion.

One institution's orientation included a walk through the spaces where student graduation would be held, and students participated in a visioning exercise, imagining whom they would invite, what accomplishments they would celebrate, and the classmates, most of whom the students would have just met, who would be there to share in the joy.

A note of caution, despite best efforts on the part of the institutional leaders and organizers, do not be discouraged by modest attendance at orientation. The adage, "Life happens" rings true for the New Majority in ways that higher-education administrators cannot foresee. Thus, many adult- and continuing-education units supplement face-to-face programs with an online version that newly admitted students can attend "live" or view a recorded version when their time permits. The aim in the student-centered environment is to remove internal barriers and provide opportunities for access.

TEACHING ADULT LEARNERS

The New Majority has pushed higher education to acknowledge diversity in learning styles and delivery modalities. The key themes are to understand diversity and characteristics of learners, to be prepared to tailor information to meet the needs of diverse learners, and to provide immediate and direct feedback.

Here's a personal story. In 1981, I taught first grade in a parochial grade school in one of the poorest parishes in Philadelphia. With no training in education, my main credentials were a degree in sociology and the fact of having been a product of the parochial system both grade school and high school. How hard could it be to manage teaching phonics, arithmetic, and religion, especially with the support of an experienced grade partner, who had more than twenty years' teaching experience but no degree? Together we were a great pair. We found that the wisdom and structure she brought to the day and the school year to meet outcomes, coupled with my openness and joy to let the children "teach" me worked to the benefit of all.

Of course, there were a range of learners. Some had foundational reading, writing, and mathematics skills, whereas others were just beginning to recognize and apply these skills. Some were incapable of sitting in their desk for even a few moments, and others were very much at ease being given an assignment to complete quietly at their desk for an extended period. By the end of a month, it seemed that options were either finding a way to "let them learn" or writing a letter of resignation. I opted for the former.

Over the school year, instructional time was limited to very short periods of time and featured a range of applications for the children. At times, it seemed like wrangling order out of chaos: students were always moving, and there seemed to be a constant hum in the class.

Real joy came during parent–teacher conferences. Nervousness soon turned to excitement as a range of parents described how their children were sounding out words to read sentences and short stories. They described how their children were engaging in "adult" conversations and were curious. This teaching-and-learning experience was transformative and directly applied to teaching adults.

Fast forward to this same instructor given her first evening school class to teach. At age twenty-four, all the students were older than me and had full-time jobs and life experiences beyond my imagination. Ironically, the course was Sociology and Social Problems; what could my classroom training teach them about their lived experiences? I quickly learned that by engaging my discipline and my students in the context of "where the students were," learning could occur.

The syllabus distributed during the initial class meeting was updated/changed/edited multiple times during the semester to meet the needs of the class and to create as much space and time as possible for the students to lead discussions through their interests and experience. It's possible that the class may not have met all the original learning outcomes or course objectives, but it's certain that the students engaged with concepts and theories in a way that was much more personal than what might have been previously imagined for them.

These early teaching experiences and the environment that emerged fall under the learning theory of andragogy. Andragogy, according to Knowles, is the science of adult learning; whereas, pedagogy has been described as the art and science of teaching children.[3] The focus of the teacher in andragogy is to facilitate an active learning environment that supports the learner's self-actualization. This compares to the theory of pedagogy, which places emphasis on the delivery of content and information from teacher to student.

Although this latter style has been the norm for several hundred years in undergraduate higher education, "disruptions" associated with instructional design for eLearning and meeting the needs of the New Majority adult student have contributed to advancing faculty development in andragogy (see for example and excellent video tutorial by Penn State World Campus Online Faculty Development).[4]

TECHNOLOGY AND SUPPORT SERVICES

A customer-service model is well suited to creating a student-centered environment for the New Majority student. This may include multimodal touch points, ranging from extended office and counter hours to technology-enhanced chat forums or ticket queues, to meet the range of student needs within a timely response period.

In addition to providing a timely and accurate response to student needs, it is important to recognize how the New Majority student uses mobile technology. Mobile technology is well suited to meet the needs of time-impoverished adult students; consequently, it is important for institutions to invest in these areas. When it comes to technology support, access and opportunity to receive timely and accurate assistance are the critical factors. Thus, the New Majority student may be best served by the implementation of an information technology call center to assist throughout the day and the year.

MEASURING SATISFACTION, SUCCESS, AND PERSISTENCE: LIFE IS IN SESSION

A student-centered environment aims to build a culture to support the goals of student satisfaction, student success, and persistence. A full understanding of the factors involved in these must account for the complex interplay of personal, institutional, community, and social environmental factors. Having objective outcomes are important guideposts for measuring institutional success, yet these measuring rods must value the diversity of students' goals represented by the New Majority.

"Being invited" is a theme that underpins each of these for the New Majority student, but in many cases, our institutions of higher education have failed to "invite" adult students to participate in customary institutional practices. For example, paper-and-pencil, end-of-the-semester course evaluations have been limited to traditional brick-and-mortar, fifteen-week semester course; whereas, the New Majority student is likely to be enrolled in an accelerated or online class. The New Majority student desires to be invited to give feedback on the course and their experience.

Persistence to graduation is a goal for the New Majority student; their journey, however, may include multiple stops and starts. At a recent baccalaureate commencement exercise, the student speaker shared that some people have looked at her as a failure because she started, stopped, and started college ten times. She went to on exclaim, "But I say that I am a winner—because I stand before you having completed my degree!"

Persistence is an area in which institutions of higher education can have a positive impact on the academic experiences of the New Majority. There is a movement underway to provide individualized wraparound services, where advisors and student support specialists collaboratively work with the student to develop an academic plan of study and academic coaching. These practices have proven highly successful to advancing persistence. Providing consistent and accurate information regarding course scheduling, degree-completion pathways, or connecting students with meaningful institutional supports have a huge impact on persistence for the New Majority.

A colleague at Saint Joseph's University, Dr. Nancy Komada, commented that on learning of a student who has not reregistered for classes, she calls or e-mails the student. How a student "steps out" is important because at some time in the future, their goal may be to return to college—whether at Saint Joseph's or elsewhere.

She reminds them to arrange for payment of any outstanding bills and encourages them to speak with any professors where they may have outstanding work so that they can receive a grade. Typically, she says, whatever has caused the adult student to take a break from studies is taking a priority, and they frequently do not realize that these steps, though small, can have a significant impact on future enrollment. By following these simple practices, most students will have an "invitation" to return in good standing.

EMERGING ISSUES

There are three emerging areas that deserve focus: collaboration and partnerships, competency-based learning, and the adaptive capacity of faculty in higher education. Since the early 1940s, the growth and expansion of higher education in the United States has been tied to the legacy of the adult- and continuing-education units of the institution. Collaboration and partnerships with local industry, connectivity between curricula and employment trends, and service in the public good are ways that the New Majority will continue to have a positive effect on the strategic vision of fiscally responsible colleges and universities.

The second issue, competency-based learning, may well represent the next disruptive innovation to impact higher education. Characteristics of a competency-based learning environment include evaluating and measuring a student on the knowledge and skills that he or she can master and demonstrate, rather than the number of seat hours (i.e., that equates to a credit hour) they have spent at the institution. And although to date, competency-based learning has been limitedly applied beyond adult-focused degree-completion programs, the success of Western Governors University, which is accredited by the Northwest Commission on Colleges and Universities, has paved the way for expanded implementation of evidence-based practices, assessment, and implementation across the globe.

The final issue, the adaptive capacity of faculty to meet the New Majority student in the context of the student's life, is going to influence whether a college or university will successfully create a student-centered learning environment. The academic experience of the New Majority student hinges on the buy-in from faculty to adapt teaching and learning modalities that align with this student population.

Following the sociological schema of the adaptation life cycle, what we see happening across many college and university campuses has been a collaborative movement between long-time adult and evening college faculty and the innovators and early adopters of eLearning to buy-in to the New Majority learning modality. In kind, the emergence and evolution of "Centers for Teaching Excellence" and faculty professional development has brought together these folks with the full faculty. To date, anecdotal accounts suggest that a minority of faculty desire to work in this realm, but best to learn this before getting in to the classroom. For those of us who do choose this route, the work is transformative.

So what end do we seek in designing student-centered structures and services? Rick Osborn, then Association for Continuing Higher Education (ACHE) president-elect, in his 2008 address to the association, summarizes it well in the following:

> This is what we do. We take students who have limited access to traditional higher education, and we transform them into an educated citizenry. We take unemployed, unskilled, and underemployed workers and transform them into a productive workforce. We take entry-level employees, young professionals, and mid-level managers, and transform them into executives and leaders. We take practicing professionals and provide training that keeps them licensed and up-to-date. We take immigrants and transform them into citizens. We take folks in transition from one life stage to another and transform them to the next.[5]

NOTES

1. Marion Bowl (2001), "Experiencing the barriers: Non-traditional students entering higher education." *Research Papers in Education* 16, no. 2: 141–160. doi: 10.1080/02671520110037410.

2. Michael Wonacott (2001), *Adult students: Recruitment and retention.* ERIC Clearinghouse on Adult and Career and Vocational Education. Practice Application Brief, no. 18. Retrieved April 25, 2017, from www. http://eric.ed.gov/?id=ED457405

3. Malcolm Knowles (1980), *The Modern Practice of Adult Education: Andragogy versus Pedagogy* (Englewood Cliffs, NJ: Prentice Hall/Cambridge).

4. Penn State University, *Online Faculty Development*. Retrieved April 25, 2017, from http://wcfd.psu.edu/programs/courses/

5. Richard Osborn (2008), Unlocking the Transformational Power of Continuing Education. 70th Annual Meeting of the Association for Continuing Higher Education

6. Retrieved April 25, 2017, http://www.acheinc.org/Resources/Documents/Proceedings/2008_proceedings.pdf

FOUR

Fit-Fear-Focus: Developing Learners' Sense of Belonging, Security, and Hope

Marguerite Weber

Models for student success have long considered the effects of students' precollege characteristics on their persistence and goal attainment; for New Majority learners, some of the most common characteristics center on anticipatory socialization (knowledge of and planning for college), socioeconomic status (to the degree that it impacts college choice), and prior academic experience (especially for returning students with some college, no degree).[1] As explored in the previous chapters by Malm, Sereni, and Griffin, three common precollege experiences for New Majority learners relate to their college-going circumstances.

1. Because of family or other circumstances, some high schoolers never imagined they would go to college, so they didn't acquire a broad scope of understanding of college-going processes. When they eventually decide to attend, they will likely choose an institution based on economic factors or convenience so they can continue to work while in school. Therefore, even though they may not have the outward appearance of New Majority learners, they likely need effective transition experiences to feel a sense of fit at the institution.
2. Others delayed entering higher education and acquired not only substantial work and life experiences but also substantial competing responsibilities and priorities. As before, they often center their choice of program on access and career benefit, but they also value

connection to other older students. Their life experiences likely developed qualities associated with persistence, including empathy and self-regulation; however, the fear of failure, of forcing family members to make sacrifices while they pursue their goals, and of coming up short in imagined classroom competition with younger, more prepared students can make them cautious and risk avoidant.

3. Many stopped out of higher education at least once and often many times. Stop-out choice may have centered on academic challenges, personal conflicts, gaps in financial resources, or even the opportunity to seize a valuable alternative experience. They are wary "shoppers" and are looking with scrutiny to the on-boarding processes (i.e., financial aid, advising, registration, orientation) and to the quality of the learning experience. Moreover, they too want access and ease in managing multiple responsibilities. Spurred by a specific goal, often career related but nearly as often to finish what they started, they seek a high-value experience that is tailored and respectful and will not tolerate activities and policies that fall short of recruitment promises.

Just as understanding New Majority learners' life circumstances is essential to support their initial commitment to attend, having insight into how New Majority students find meaningful ways to be engaged helps an institution to craft high-impact learning experiences. New Majority learners, even those with professional success, are often concerned that they lack the will and skill to negotiate complex college systems. A transition experience anticipates these concerns and provides just-in-time guidance, support, and affirmation.

Student success requires both the students' efforts and the institution's resources and services. Student and institutional success depend on an environment that fosters participation and removes barriers to students' realizing benefits.

Although today's students have a longing for connection to engaging and satisfying learning, the complexities of modern life provide multiple competitors for their time, energy, and good will. This proves especially true for New Majority learners, who have a practical bent and personal focus to their educational investments; they have little patience for engagement activities that don't connect specifically to their present lives and future goals.

The Fit-Fear-Focus model[2] was developed through work with urban high school students and adult learners engaged in college-readiness programming. It describes the continuous decision-making framework for persistence and departure in higher education, and importantly, identifies cohesive retention strategies institutions can adapt to respond to the students' needs. The initial framework has been tested and refined in work at community colleges and universities. It is framed as a call-and-response spiritual: students call out their questions and their longing, and a successful institution will need to be prepared to respond through multiple channels. In this way, Fit-Fear-Focus is both a way of understanding retention and assessing institutional student readiness to be effective for New Majority learners.

> Fit—*Student call* (coming to understand personal values that matter): *There are people like me here. Institutional response* (in presenting targeted evidence): *People like you do well here.*
> Fear—*Student call* (after reflecting on academic ability as well as time and financial resources): *I recognize my strengths but fear my challenges will keep me from being successful. Institutional response* (in presenting relevant evidence): *Because we know you, we have the support resources to grow and celebrate your strengths and address your challenges.*
> Focus—*Student call* (as they learn to navigate processes and systems here): *I believe that the value of the learning provides a good return on my investment of money, time, energy, and good will. Institutional response* (in timely and consistent messages and activities): *We respect your investments by eliminating unnecessary barriers to your progress, and we work hard to ensure that the credential is highly relevant and valued in the community and in the workplace.*

This model, especially when used as a framework for transitional experiences, reinforces students' sense of belonging, security, and hope, which are capacities associated with student success.

Students with a sense of belonging will take risks and engage with other students. They will celebrate their transformations and generously share their experiences with newcomers to the learning environment. Students with a sense of security demonstrate resilience. They can connect their lived experience with reflections on past successes as well as times when they survived failure and can apply those perseverance habits to new tasks.

New Majority learners with a sense of hope believe that their choice to pursue an education right here and right now will be worth the needed time, energy, and goodwill. They hope to be a role model for loved ones and to reap benefits as they apply their education to new challenges.

Those preparing for New Majority learners should set priorities and assess program outcomes based on these goals:

> *Strengthen students' sense of belonging (fit):* Support a student experience that is characterized by attention to students' career and academic goals and to their meaningful personal development as they are transformed by their learning with intentional, recursive, and engaging experiences. In this way, practitioners help them to man-

age the pressure of their urgent and continuous second thoughts on the quality of their decision to attend. And an important lever in managing that stress is students' engagement with other students who are having similar pressures and making the decision to stay the course.

Strengthen students' sense of security (fear): Regardless of prior educational experiences, a student's sense of security is tied to the belief in the sufficiency of personal resources (knowledge, skills, abilities, time, energy, goodwill, social support, and financial support) to attain their goals and to overcome barriers to success. When threats to that security come from immediate or anticipated resource shortfalls, students need timely, accurate, responsive support and help to develop persistence strategies.

Strengthen students' sense of hope (focus): Almost by definition, a student who chooses to start an educational program is driven by an abiding sense of hope. The kind of durable hope that is needed to complete a learning goal is rooted in past learning experiences and in received values. Learners calculate how difficult something will be based on their past experiences in similar situations (i.e., high school or workplace training); then they learn about what kinds of growth and change will be needed to attain the goal; finally, they weigh the needed effort, expense, and risk against the perceived value of completion.

Practitioners can influence this calculation in several ways. First, learning experiences should build students' internal resources so that the gap between what they have and what they need is narrow. And second, institutions need to be intentional in eliminating costly barriers along the way, and this smoothing the way again lowers the perceived costs and risks. Third, when there is tight alignment between programs and experiences and their postcredential–completion life experiences, students realize that the value of the end product is enhanced.

In truth, higher education must do all three. Learning activities that connect learners to each other, to the institution, and to their future goals have the promise of supporting persistence and success behaviors and raising the value of the degree program for participants.

Higher education is not without a map to navigate strategies that promote New Majority learners' sense of belonging, security, and hope. Classroom- and program-based strategies for engaging students with their learning, with one another, and with the world at large have been defined as high-impact practices (HIPs). George Kuh[3] has described a range of HIPs that have been empirically demonstrated to support students' deep learning and to increase their self-reported gains in general, personal, and practical knowledge.

Traditional HIPs include a range of curricular and cocurricular learning experiences: learning communities, collaborative projects, global learning, service/community-based learning, and culminating experiences/capstones. However, standard approaches to HIPS, like study abroad, living-learning communities, and unpaid internships can be inaccessible to historically underserved students.[4]

Increasingly, they are inaccessible to New Majority learners who may lack the "knowledge of college" that would help them to value cocurricular or out of class experiences, who may have personal management challenges to tackle more than what's absolutely required to pass a course, or who may have a combination of both. And too, because HIPs are often created to align with first-year experiences, those who have prior college won't have access to these foundational resources.

Therefore, new experiences that achieve the same outcomes but better suit students' learning circumstances must be designed. Conforming programs and services for New Majority learners to HIPs is an effective way for an institution to respond to students' Fit-Fear-Focus calls.

HIPS ADAPTED FOR NEW MAJORITY LEARNERS

A first step in focusing HIPs on the New Majority–learner experience is to ensure that the practices are high quality and engaging. American Association of Colleges and Universities (AAC&U) has developed a list of high-impact quality dimensions,[5] and Table 4.1[6] indicates approaches to adapting those quality dimensions to support the success of all students.

These good strategies apply to HIPs for all students, not just New Majority learners. However, learners who have been away from formal learning for long periods especially thrive in enriched environments characterized by respect, challenge, support, and clear and relevant value. In other words, they evoke belonging, security, and hope. Integrating the intent of traditional HIPs with the quality dimensions described, and then adapting those practices to the practicalities of New Majority learners' lives, makes possible a range of accessible adapted high-impact practices (AHIPs) that support success.

The AHIPs[7] described here were developed and implemented for a small private liberal arts university where the president had declared a guarantee that all graduates would experience at least three HIPs. Fulfilling this promise was a matter of planning and resources for the institution's traditional student base. However, for New Majority learners, both those who were increasingly entering full-time/day-time programs while balancing work and the adult part-time students in a targeted evening program, access to the benefits of the HIPs was dependent on design.

The specific constraints included a geographical area rich with competition in the form of fully online, accelerated, and hybrid programs easily

Table 4.1. High-impact practice quality dimensions

Quality Dimension	Example	Explanation
Performance expectations set at appropriately high levels	Eliminating remediation/developmental studies by offering variable-credit core courses embedded with verbal, quantitative, information, and technology literacies.	Students are challenged but supported, and they are given choices in what kinds of support services to employ.
Frequent, timely, and constructive feedback with structured opportunities to reflect on and integrate learning	A multipart assignment with feedback at each of these stages: • Content acquisition • Control of essential processes • Support for claims and premises • Integration of learning in final product	Students develop a strong sense of security with multiple low-stakes evaluations that coalesce into a higher-stakes final evaluation.
Investment of time and effort by students over an extended period	Connected assignments across linked courses, with expectations for substantive analysis, reflection, reframing, and revision.	Students demonstrate autonomy in matching effort to outcomes and experience the qualitative difference between an authentic and an artificial task.
Opportunities to discover the relevance of learning through real-world applications	Student and faculty research and professional activities fair to show authentic work products.	Students see how different disciplines solve urgent problems.
Through experiences with diversity, students learn from people whose circumstances differ	A critical consciousness endeavor in which students learn from diverse others while also offering their own expertise to others	Students understand that issues have a contextual frame that impacts and is understood by different people in different ways.
Interactions with faculty and peers about substantive matters	Shared responsibility for identifying a problem; analyzing the context and effects; developing multiple solutions; and testing to find a best-case approach.	Students experience a greater understanding of the mutually reinforcing relationship between teacher and learner.
Public demonstration of competence	The professional activities fair described would also be an example of this quality measure.	Students practice being peers with experts, reinforcing their sense of belonging and hope.

available across the region. Therefore, two primary design challenges were differentiation to find a niche population to serve in ways the other programs were not and portability to reach these niche clients across the metropolitan area. Table 4.2 provides a list of these AHIPs as well as the persistence outcomes associated with their design.

Access Pedagogy

For adults particularly, and arguably for most contemporary students, the traditional classroom tends to be an inelegant design: the faculty member's effort is out of proportion to the effort of the students, who, with constant access to information online and with experience navigating complex social systems, are both capable of and eager to take more responsibility for their learning if it means that the environment would be more customized to their goals and more respectful of their lives and experiences.

The Access Pedagogy is a product of design thinking, specifically aligning human effort (who is the best person to accomplish the essential work) with technology (how can technology support human effort and accomplish work that humans can't or shouldn't be doing) with sustainability (how can the effort-technology relationship be scaled while retaining high-quality outcomes).

The Access Pedagogy is a variation of a blended (hybrid or "flipped") learning environment. A hybrid class can benefit learners by reducing the time required to be on campus and by allowing them to spend more concentrated time with reading and writing assignments. However, New Majority learners, especially those who have been out of formal education for long periods, may need more directed guidance in using the technology and in prioritizing tasks.

Fully online (OL) courses provide learners with complete freedom in how to allot their time; however, many have made the choice to return to college not only to get a degree but also to form new connections with others. They often have an idealized image of college in mind, and learn-

Table 4.2. Adapted high-impact practices and outcomes

Adapted HIPs	Learning Outcomes	Persistence Outcomes
Access Pedagogy	Deep learning	Active and collaborative learning
Divergent thinking to solve wicked problems	Practical and personal knowledge	Level of academic challenge
Prior learning, competency learning assessment, contracts	General, practical, and personal knowledge	Supportive campus environment

ing in a classroom is part of that vision. The Access Pedagogy draws on the best of both face-to-face (F2F) and OL designs and then adds two additional values: connection and self-direction.

The main difference is that faculty members inhabit the OL environment, and learning mentors inhabit the F2F space. Faculty in paired courses collaborate on the actions that happen in the learning mentor-supported F2F sessions and ensure that the instruction shows how the learning in the two courses can be integrated and mutually supporting. The learning mentor helps to make space for higher quality faculty interactions: those focused on how experts use the subject, what they find beautiful and useful in this way of seeing the world, and how students can be engaged as potential future colleagues who also celebrate and refine this disciplinary knowledge.

Here is how the model works. Start with the amount of effort available. Typically, in a F2F class, an instructor meets with the students for approximately three hours a week and tells students to "study" for two hours for every hour in the classroom, or a total of nine hours a week. In the Access model, designers divided the nine-hour a week commitment into three spaces: OL, self-directed learning, and F2F.

In the OL environment (with an expectation of three hours per week of student engagement), the instructor is responsible for clarifying expectations, directing students to resources, explaining how experts use those resources, and checking students' understanding as they use them. The instructor relates the learning to the students' goals and to professional expectations beyond the classroom, provides sustained formative and summative feedback to support the learners' growth, and conducts assessments/grading activities.

In the self-directed time (what might otherwise be "studying" for three hours per week), the learner engages with the resources, completes assignments, and responds to faculty feedback.

In the Access Pedagogy, the F2F environment, roughly three hours a week shared between the two intentionally linked courses, focuses on what in a traditional class would be called "homework." In a traditional class, homework typically provides an opportunity to check students' emerging understanding through low-risk, low-point-value tasks. In the Access Pedagogy, the connected activities provide for just-in-time formative feedback from the learning mentor and peers and multiple opportunities to apply the learning in authentic situations.

The active learning experiences in the F2F sessions achieve the same goals as traditional homework: complete low-risk, low-point-value tasks that provide opportunities for the faculty member, in collaboration with the learning mentor to check learners' emerging understanding. It's homework, but it's in our "house"—the classroom—and it is guided and facilitated by the learning mentor, not the faculty member.

The learning mentor is responsible for facilitating the F2F sessions and coaches the students in how to use technology tools to discover, organize, and communicate information and in how to adapt those tools to work and life responsibilities. When the faculty members use technology to come into the F2F session, they observe and assess student learning and guide reflections on the connections between the course learning and life experiences and goals. In this way, learners develop strategies to be successful in subsequent accelerated and online courses and learn how to connect to communities of learners in and out of the classroom.

Intentional efforts to promote active engagement with and among New Majority learners, as described previously, is also good androgogical practice (i.e., pedagogy of success for adult learners). Students who have been working or caring for the family all day or all week can come to a classroom where they do more than sit and listen or sit and talk. They move around the room, find and use resources, and connect their learning to their lives and goals. They can use their maturity and leadership in the classroom and experience working in highly effective teams to reflect on social and work issues.

Divergent Thinking to Solve Wicked Problems

A powerful traditional HIP is engagement with global learning focused on developing in students a sense of perspective, openness, and intercultural competence.[8] Students learn to reflect on their own values and perspectives and gain personal knowledge through that process of critical reflection and engaging in big questions that arise when they discover a world of difference. This can be a means to not only celebrate personal strengths and differences but also develop new abilities and perspectives to carry forward.

The AHIP of activities focused on divergent thinking to resolve wicked problems is an approach that resonates with New Majority learners because it respects their life experiences and provides relevant challenges that connect to their future goals. Through divergent thinking activities, student can learn the forms of self-reflection and critical analyses that might be parallel to the deep introspection and connection they engage in when participating in more traditional HIPs, like study abroad and service learning.

Atherton[9] explains that divergent thinking is a process of discovering multiple resolutions of a paradox (solutions to a problem, opportunities to use an object in new ways, entrepreneurial approaches to meeting a need, etc.). For example, an instructor might incorporate the "uses of objects test" in which participants are given a common object (e.g., a paper clip, a pencil, a blanket). First, they work individually to list all possible uses of the object. Then students work in teams to develop a nonduplicative list of additional uses. Thus, students learn that more good solutions can be discovered by a team than can be discovered alone.

The uses-of-object activity then leads to more and more complex critical consciousness activities that encourage learners to reflect on the limits of their knowing, on a wider world of diverse perspectives, and on strategies to ask for help and to respect others' points of view and values. In addition, this practice can promote students' perceptions of greater academic challenge because they will learn to take risks and seek help, knowing they can rely on habits of critical and creative thinking and on others who will help them to continue to learn.

Divergent thinking activities can be adapted across the curriculum with overt connections to insights about the power of diversity in high-functioning teams. They are particularly successful when incorporated with opportunities to practice fast (intuitive) and slow (deliberative) thinking[10] and to experience how to employ diverse thinking strategies when solving complex problems. By focusing on a range of thinking strategies, learners practice identifying and analyzing their assumptions and come to think critically about the strength of those assumptions.[11]

Here is an example of task sequence that requires divergent thinking, fast and slow thinking, and appreciating global perspectives. In a Global Leadership course using this AHIP, students select a world region and focus their individual and collaborative assignments on perspectives from that region. To prepare for a culminating presentation, they engage in a linked series of research-based activities.

- *Task 1 (fast thinking):* Think of a cross-cultural mistake you have experienced, and discuss the outcome and what should have been done in that instance.
- *Task 2 (slow thinking):* On of the Internet, one can interact with people who are different in cultural background. Explain the cross-cultural pitfalls that exist when communicating through the Internet, and describe the etiquette and ethics that should be applied when engaging in this electronic intercultural communication with significant groups in your region.
- *Task 3 (slow thinking):* Based on your research and your team discussions, teach the class about how the culture of your region would define an effective leader. After reflections on all the class lessons on leadership through the cultural frameworks of the regions are presented, analyze which characteristics of leadership seem to be universal across the cultures and which are specific to the culture of your researched region. Provide credible evidence and examples.
- *Task 4 (culminating task):* Identify what you feel are the two key cultural characteristics that could produce the greatest uncertainty for a multinational enterprise (MNE) entering your region/country for the first time, and explain why these two characteristics would

produce the greatest risk. Based on your findings, propose a strategy for that MNE to mitigate and control these risks.

As with the Access Pedagogy described, students are put into learning situations that start with their current intuitive assumptions that shape their perceptions of their personal, family, civic, and work cultures and are then moved to more deliberative examinations of their perspectives as culturally constructed. Their experiences with faculty in these situations are characterized by the DEEP principles of "talent development," that is, meeting "students where they are in terms of their academic and social developmental and then [working] hard to empower students to achieve without regard to starting level."[12]

Prior Learning, Competency Learning Assessment, and Contracts

It may seem odd to equate alternative credit assessment with an experience as impactful as an internship; however, when accomplished with an intentional plan to connect the experience to Liberal Education and America's Promise (LEAP) and persistence outcomes,[13] this practice can promote the habit of making connections among areas of general, practical, and personal knowledge and can give students a sense that the campus community is supportive of students' success goals.

For example, in a portfolio development course, students develop an understanding of learning theory, cognitive development, metacognition, and effective communications. Specifically, they move through a process of evaluating their work experience from the perspective of what they learned, how they learned it, what learning strategies are particularly effective, and how they self-regulate when challenged to learn new things. They learn about the role of motivation and self-efficacy in determining what kinds of learning goals will command their attention and lead to expending resources.

Thus, students develop a habit of connecting their past learning to the present degree program requirements. In addition, the course demands technological literacy and quantitative reasoning. They represent their learning and their achievements through a range of graphic organizers and presentation tools, and they assess the value of their achievements using research on career field rewards, productivity measures, and returns on investments.

Finally, students are led through activities that connect their experiences in the degree program to future goals. In cooperation with academic advisors, learners create a completion plan and learning contract for additional experiential and cocurricular learning that can help them plan to be lifelong learners. The student maps out learning, academic, and career goals and develops a habit of scanning for, completing, and reflecting on opportunities that arise in and out the classroom, in and out of work and in their personal, civic, and family lives.

These future-facing practices and the networking opportunities that come from meeting learning goals on the contract can be a means to meet the goals of an internship without the time commitment that adult learners may find to be a barrier. The value-added of the portfolio approach and its integration into the degree completion plan is that students gain practice measuring the productivity behaviors that are valued across multiple industries.

The high quality of the interactions, through the portfolio course, the portfolio review, and the degree completion map, conveys a solid sense of a supportive campus environment. One learner engaged in this process declared, "I feel like I got the golden ticket!" She had shopped numerous adult programs and found that the combinations of supports, culminating in this portfolio process, most closely fit her sense of what she needed to be successful.

CONCLUSION

Although there is merit in building New Majority programs anew, as was done at this particular institution, AHIPs can be incorporated into existing programs singly or in stages, but there must be collaboration and coordination between program administrators, faculty, and support staff. It starts with a clear commitment to ensuring consistency in the quality of student-learning experiences for all learners, including older, part-time, and commuter students. Because, as Finley and McNair confirm, these students and other historically underrepresented learners who now represent the New Majority in higher education, often lack access to traditional HIP, and nontraditional practices are needed.[14]

The approach is a kind of reverse engineering, starting with the outcomes that matter for deep learning, broad learning, and personal learning and those that encourage students' commitment to completion. Program designers then reimagine ways to use the resources to capture the unique values proposition of the institution.

Access to high-quality opportunities to earn a college degree is increasingly becoming a social justice issue. In a world where the consequences of not having postsecondary education or training are increasingly dire, it is the responsibility of learning institutions to reduce barriers to access and to increase the likelihood of success, even for students who may come to college lacking academic preparation in foundational skills, who need to balance employment with school and family responsibilities, and who have other life complications that distract from their ability to focus fully on the demands of school.

It's not enough simply to change the times of traditional courses and cocurricular offerings or to shift to fully OL environments so that New Majority learners can be there. If we don't fundamentally change those experiences while ensuring high-quality outcomes, we aren't doing everything we can to invite success.

NOTES

1. Braxton, Hirschy, and McClendon, 2004.
2. Marguerite Weber (2015), "Promoting Adult Learner Success through Adapted High Impact Practices," In *2015 Sourcebook*, Consortium for Student Retention Data Exchange (Norman: University of Oklahoma Press).
3. George D. Kuh (2008), *High-Impact Educational Practices: What They Are, Who Has Access to Them, and Why They Matter* (Washington, D.C.: American Association of Colleges and Universities).
4. A. Finley and T. McNair (2013), *Assessing Underserved Students' Engagement in High Impact Practices* (Washington, D.C.: American Association of Colleges and Universities).
5. Center for Engaged Learning (n.d.), *Internships*. Retrieved October 4, 2016, from http://www.centerforengagedlearning.org/doing-engaged-learning/internships/#impact-practices
6. Adapted from Community College of Baltimore County (2015), "High Impact Practices." Workshop presented at the 7th Annual Maryland Association of Community Colleges (MACC) Completion Summit, November.
7. Marguerite Weber (2014), "Design for Student Success: Lessons Learned, Continuous Improvements Needed," In *2014 Sourcebook*, Consortium for Student Retention Data Exchange (Norman, OK: University of Oklahoma Press).
8. American Association of Colleges and Universities (2013), *High Impact Practices*. Retrieved July 10, 2017, from https://www.aacu.org/resources/high-impact-practices.
9. J. S. Atherton (2013), *Learning and Teaching: Convergent and Divergent Learning*. Retrieved June 5, 2015, from http://www.learningandteaching.info/learning/converge.htm
10. D. Kahnemann (2011), *Thinking Fast and Slow* (New York, NY: Farrar, Straus, & Giroux).
11. Brookfield, 2013, p. 35.
12. W. R. Habley, J. L. Bloom, and S. Robbins. (2012). *Increasing Persistence: Research-Based Strategies for College Student Success* (San Francisco, CA: Jossey-Bass), 111.
13. American Association of Colleges and Universities, *High Impact Practices*.
14. Finley and McNair, *Assessing Underserved Students' Engagement in High Impact Practices*.

FIVE

Technology: Higher-Education Disruption and New Majority–Learner Access

Paul Walsh

Higher education has been transformed by technology. Faculty and students alike rely on technology to distribute and gather information and assess the efficiency of the retention and success of the dissemination. Student information systems manage the transactional business of the institution. Libraries no longer have card catalogs. The school athletic center has card-swipe access and heart rate monitors on treadmills. The classroom has evolved and, along with dozens of other campus units, has even moved online.

There are more than seven thousand titles at the Library of Congress dealing with technology in higher education. Two hundred and sixty-three million Google results also detail the obvious; technology has been incredibly disruptive in higher education. In *The Innovative University: Changing the DNA of Higher Education from the Inside Out*,[1] Christensen and Eyring describe how accreditation teams in the mid-1990s reacted with skepticism to some online innovations. Hindsight may make us somewhat forgetful that the technology transformation of the last two decades has been wrought with varying levels of cynicism and uncertainty.

Some technologies changed the face of teaching and learning, some were merged or bought out, and some did not survive. Many universities had to change their technology solutions as the marketplace saw tools like Horizon Wimba, WebCT, and Angel merge into the Blackboard suite. Universities built virtual campuses in *Second Life* expecting students to virtually fly in to attend courses. The gradebook tool *Knack* and the lesson plan and collaboration site Collabo never reached enough mass to sustain business.[2]

Technology has touched every area of campus life, if not in primary function then in administrative ones. Five areas where technology has been a game changer, especially for burgeoning populations of New Majority learners, include classroom technology, online education, student information systems, data analytics, and enrollment.

The campus classroom may still look like its industrial-age ancestor, but the technology in the room offers incredible levels of sophistication. Blackboards are long gone; whiteboards are likely next in line for extinction. Projectors are commonplace but are slowly being replaced with touch-sensitive, flat-screen monitors. This is much more than just using PowerPoint; it is flipped classrooms, streaming media, lecture capture, video conferencing, assistive technology, and thousands of dollars of equipment that make each classroom into a technology hub. The technology-enhanced learning space has transformed how information is delivered, received, shared, and stored.

Online education fought a much steeper climb. From the beginning, teaching and learning online were compared to the traditional classroom. The prominent learning management system named itself Blackboard to connote classroom teaching. However, quality concerns plagued online learning from the start, and some faculty resisted. Supporters claimed comparisons to be unfair because online learning was being held to a different scrutiny level than teaching in the classroom.

The benefits of learning online and guidance from organizations like Quality Matters (QM) and Online Learning Consortium (OLC) eventually outweighed resistance, as evaluation tools were developed to assess student engagement, student productivity, and student-learning outcomes. Of course, as with most technologies, room for improvement remains.

Student information systems like Oracle's PeopleSoft and Ellucian's Banner go back to the late 1980s and have eventually expanded their presence in higher education to include financial, human resources, customer-relations management, and enterprise-resource planning. As administrative systems, they are at times reviled by faculty for being overly inflexible, bureaucratic, and expensive. They are also indispensable. Universities may unbundle some of these tools in the future, and open-source tools like Odoo and Kuali may gain more users, but the fact remains that these technologies have transformed the business of higher education.

Data analytics have only recently reached a tipping point in colleges and universities. What was once the purview of only a few well-staffed institutional research centers is now available in dashboards of gauges, charts, and graphs. Tweaking institutional intervention strategies to impact retention and student success, particularly when there are achievement gaps with demographics of New Majority learners, has only just begun to impact the higher-education landscape.

Enrollment-management technologies include admissions marketing, pricing and financial aid, institutional-response strategies, and retention programs. Incoming students may still receive a deluge of mail from prospective schools, but texting students from an enrollment-management system is likely to get more responses. These technologies track interest, SATs and grades, visits, and just about any level of contact a school would have with a prospective student. They are instrumental in recruiting, funding, tracking, retaining students, and in setting enrollment strategies.

Technology will continue to transform how colleges and universities conduct business and teach. The New Media Consortium identifies five important developments in educational technology for higher education in their most recent report:[3]

- Bring your own device (BYOD)
- Learning analytics and adaptive learning
- Augmented and virtual reality
- Makerspaces
- Affective computing

These prognostications follow a one- to five-year horizon, but faculty might have a hard time relating to virtual reality and makerspaces in this technology forecast. Changing this to more of a "local forecast" for faculty and students, this list could be adapted to

- Data
- Textbooks
- Online learning (continued)
- Teams and roles
- Changing the ways students think

The statement, "If we can't measure it, you can't manage it"[4] is attributed to management guru Peter Drucker. Higher education, informed by Drucker's logic, has been gaining momentum and success in developing responsive assessments to measure student learning. Within the assessment process, the role of the faculty member becomes more intimate and valued by students if the measures are focused on specific and timely feedback that directs learning, personalizes education, and makes data a partner in a student's progression.

From this perspective, competency-based education (CBE) can work in more than the science, technology, engineering, and mathematics (STEM) fields and can lead to higher-order thinking like interpretation, analysis, and synthesis. As applications of CBE expand, there will be a need for more and earlier assessment of student learning and goals and for data sharing between courses that don't prejudice a faculty member but rather inform and empower the faculty to have the intended impact and help students build competencies.

Textbooks are not done evolving. This is a multibillion dollar industry that is ripe for disruption. Most books now come with online content that is interactive and includes assignments and grades. These features will not be enough to prevent the inevitable. Although Napster didn't kill the music industry, it was a herald of a digital revolution that has totally changed how consumers get their music. Open educational resources and low- or no-cost books may not be the end of specialized content found in the upper division and graduate school, but the democratization of general education content is likely.

Higher education has not seen the end of change in online education, which allows learners to access content at their convenience. Most online courses have been text heavy and asynchronous, and only a few schools have an online footprint that is drastically outside of their time zone. Emerging trends include synchronous, live interactive courses that include video and user data so every click can be captured and analyzed.

Massive open online courses (MOOCs) aren't the "end of higher education" as headlines of 2013 professed, but they are not done by any stretch. They may have fallen off the Gartner "hype cycle,"[5] but their potential to deliver high-education content remains. As we develop means to assess individual and team learning in MOOCs, through students' self-reported gains and through other measures, MOOCs have the potential to earn a place in formal credentialing.

The most significant change for online education will be the unbundling of the traditional learning-management system (LMS). Higher education has followed an approach that placed all services under one umbrella with Learning Tools Interoperability (LTI), setting a standard for how third-party tools could plug into platforms like Blackboard. The LMS of the future will be more of a confederation of tools specific to the course than a central operating system that manages every course across the spectrum of programs and learners.

It isn't just the technology that will change. The roles of faculty and students will change as well. If data analytics can get to the point of measuring student learning at a fairly granular level, won't this make learning more individual, even when working in teams, participating in experiential learning, or on service projects? Peter Smith wrote in *The Quiet Crisis: How Higher Education Is Failing America*, "Imagine if every learner in a school were assessed to determine how she or he learns best, and the results—a learning profile—traveled with the learner so each teacher could match pedagogy and curriculum to the learner. Quality, speed, and value of learning would skyrocket."[6]

Learning analytics can help identify potential problems in an academic program, or elsewhere in the student experience, that adversely affects student success. As analytics and assessment become more immediate, it will change how the student interacts with the content and with the faculty. This immediacy may be enabled by technological advances in grading, not removing the need for a faculty member, but certainly changing it. Machine grading isn't going to be the Scantron sheets that have been around for decades; it will be AI that is capable of norming with faculty standards.

Randy Bass, vice provost for education and professor of English at Georgetown University, leads the Designing the Future initiative and was the founding director of the Center for New Designs in Learning and Scholarship (CNDLS). In "Disrupting Ourselves: The Problem of Learning in Higher Education," Bass envisions not only the changing role of the faculty and learner but also of an entire team. Instead of placing the instructor at the center in a "hub-and-spoke model," Bass posits a team-based design consisting of instructional designers, writing specialists, librarians with information technology expertise, instructional technologists, and faculty working together.

The team-based model asks not only how all of these instructional experts might collaborate with faculty on a new design but also how some of them (e.g., embedded librarians) might play a role in the delivery of the course so that not all of the burden of the expanded instructional model falls on the instructor; this model focuses on changing course structures so that faculty will be empowered and supported in an expanded approach to teaching as a result of teaching these courses.[7]

What does this change mean for the New Majority learner? How will they be challenged or benefit from this technology-driven shift in higher education?

Joanne Cleaver's 2012 work *The Career Lattice: Combat Brain Drain, Improve Company Culture, and Attract Top Talent* presented the idea that U.S. workers need to be far more flexible, proficient, and professionally connected than in previous years.[8] No longer would people move up the career ladder within an organization, instead, they will move from job to job. Indeed, the Bureau of Labor Statistics estimates that the average baby boomer (born in the years 1957 to 1964) will hold an average of 11.7 jobs.[9]

This lateral/diagonal movement between positions presents multiple challenges because learners will maintain employment and enter and reenter higher education to keep up their skills and competencies. Higher education will need to serve this population with programs embedded with transferable skills, particularly in technology.

We know it is a false assumption that millennial students are "digital natives" with special powers to access and integrate information from online sources because differences in economic status, geographical locations, and the wealth of school systems result in uneven access to technology and its benefits. Similarly, it is dangerous to assume that adult learners already have technology skills because they are coming from the workplace.

Conversely, an adult learner's technical skills might be highly specialized. A forty-three-year old sergeant with considerable technology proficiencies in the military may find transition to a new career daunting. Higher education may not make that move easier when only offering a single-threaded approach to technology associated with a degree program.

Patricia Cranton's foundational work on adult learners, *Understanding and Promoting Transformative Learning: A Guide for Educators of Adults*,[10] challenges educators to "let the soul speak" when working with learners who are insecure, lacking in confidence, anxious, or unsupported to overcome potential barriers. Although Cranton doesn't include current terms like *risk metrics* and *data analysis*, she clearly understood that potential barriers for the New Majority learner were habits, beliefs, and concerns that students bring to the classroom as well as those they left behind at home and work.

Background, individual characteristics, and environmental factors are identified by Joann Horton as the three constructs most "essential to readiness and success as they reflect subject-matter mastery, general work attitude, and effective career decision-making, respectively."[11] As presented in chapter 1 (see Figure 1.2), New Majority learners have complex responsibilities: jobs, parents and children to take care of, transportation issues, making dinner, and studying all revolve around the most valuable commodity in a learner's life—time.

Technology in higher education does not always deliver on its promise of making things easier and saving time. Too often, the New Majority learner must navigate a Department of Motor Vehicles approach to student services and technology. Few administrators, and even fewer faculty, know the intricacies of the business and technical process students encounter from initial inquiry through matriculation and graduation.

How easy is it to register, pay bills, renew a library book, or to obtain a parking permit or even to complete a course evaluation at most universities? How easy is it for the New Majority learner who needs to get off from work, secure child care, and navigate a maze of unconnected business and technical systems before campus offices close? Those who persevere make it to the classroom where technology may present a similar challenge.

And even faculty members share traits with New Majority learners when they engage the rapid changes in technology that impact their work and lives. Higher educators are experts in their fields, rising to the pinnacle of knowledge in a select field. This specialized training does not always include becoming an expert in pedagogies of engagement or innovative technologies.

For students, universities include technical competencies when mapping general education competencies. However, many New Majority learners have been swirling in and out of higher education as they pursue their degree goals and may transfer in with some credit or return to college as they work their way up and across the career lattice; thus, they may miss these technical competencies.

What the New Majority learner needs is for higher education to create a scaffolded, transferable skill set of technological competencies that go beyond the first year and the vertical program to extend into multiple aspects of the student experience, curricular and cocurricular.

Higher education has not missed the boat entirely. As described previously, technology has been transformative. Yet, there is a danger in approaching technology as only a tool without considering the user.

Compare this approach as seen in two aspects of the modern university: the library and online learning. Counterintuitively, it is the library that has adapted and pivoted to meet the needs of students, including the adult learner. Technology is at the foundation of how both these campus units operate, but on most campuses only one is situated to serve students. Libraries in the twenty-first century are nearly virtual, but they have positioned themselves to do more than collect and preserve resources. Libraries provide a welcome environment and genuine support for learning, research, and discovery. Too often, the online learning unit provides only the technology or minimal training (the "click here" approach) to learn a tool like an LMS.

Libraries have had to evolve to remain relevant. They have added technology, built partnerships within academic departments, and scaled services to support teaching and research. Look at the library's approach to reserve materials. What once was a shelf behind the reservation desk transformed into e-reserves and streaming media.

In Pete McDonnell's *The Experiential Library: Transforming Academic and Research Libraries through the Power of Experiential Learning*,[12] Jayne Blodgett from the University of Northern Colorado details how libraries are essential to the academic mission, working on service learning, engagement, and social justice. In 2013, Blodgett offered a first year seminar program titled "Beyond Shushing: Libraries and Literacy in the 21st Century." The faculty–librarian teaches on campus, leads embedded information technologies and research workshops for students, pilots new pedagogical approaches, and helps students build transferable skills.

Where is the online learning unit at most campuses? Is it a technical solution or an academic entity? As mentioned in chapter 1, 28 percent of students take at least one online course. Why is it that universities see online learning as a strategic imperative (63.3 percent of chief academic leaders say that online learning is critical to their long-term strategy[13]) but don't take time to teach students how to be successful in this environment? It may be that many administrators and faculty older than forty years of age have never taken an online class, or it may be that higher education is used to K–12 teaching students how to learn, and so administrators assume they have had the resources to address online learning skills and habits.

The common approach is to put students into online courses and require that they spend considerable time there. This is the equivalent of pushing students, particularly adult learners with little prior experience, into the deep end and telling them that they'll learn to swim by doing laps. Conversely, how would online learning look to the New Majority learner if it had been allowed to develop along the same lines as the library? There would be online learning tutors and coaches to prepare adult learners, concierge services online in the evenings and on weekends, and embedded content liaisons that could help map transferable technology skills across all online programs.

Few schools can invest in that level of support. Elite schools with deep endowments may be more prepared to embrace technology, but those same schools serve fewer New Majority learners, for whom the innovation divide may be wider. Technology can be implemented on a shoestring budget. It can be rolled out with little to no support. It can be left to the faculty and the students to figure things out, but with students already at risk, why add the stressors?

As a practical example, how many learners who juggle work, family, and community responsibilities have the time to learn simple video editing for their next presentation, and how many schools are intentional in making this a skill to learn before graduating? PowerPoint came out in 1987, and using it to present in class is a fairly low technology expectation. If that is where the bar is set, most students, particularly the time-constrained New Majority learner, will only go that high. Faculty, similarly, will be reticent to insert media into their assignments if there are few support mechanisms for students on campus. Universities will need to address how to remain innovative and implement emerging technologies while addressing gaps, particularly in areas of support.

Technologies around higher education are rolling out faster than most technology units can support them. Campus e-mail has migrated to the cloud with providers like Google's G Suite for Education and Microsoft's Office365 offering solutions that some campuses struggle to keep up with. As *Yammer*, *Delve*, and *Sway* were included in the Office365 suite, technology offices had to decide to leave these tools open, contain them, offer support, or train the campus on their use as an academic or office tools. Unless a faculty member has experience with these tools or has a means to engage campus technology services, it may be the technology office that decides if new tools are made available.

All faculty members have a responsibility to maintain their own technology proficiency and stay up to date on technologies that could benefit their instruction or their field. A dentist who doesn't keep up on the latest technology to fight cavities will quickly lose customers. Dental technology isn't a fad—it is a part of the modern dental practice. The same is true for academics; higher education has been transformed by technology. It will continue to do so—in both subtle and drastic ways. Every practitioner needs a plan, or at minimum a genuine curiosity, for how they will encounter technology, adjust their roles as instructors, and provide the New Majority learner skills that transfer across programs and professions.

NOTES

1. C. M. Christensen and Henry J. Eyring (2011), *The Innovative University: Changing the DNA of Higher Education from the Inside Out* (San Francisco, CA: Jossey-Bass).

2. Daniel Shumski (2013), *Five Failed Start-Ups You Should Study*. Retrieved July 10, 2017, from http://www.educationdive.com/news/5-failed-education-startups-you-should-study/196134/

3. Horizon Report (2016), *2016 Higher Education Report*. Retrieved July 10, 2017, from http://cdn.nmc.org/media/2016-nmc-horizon-report-he-EN.pdf

4. Paul Zak (2013), *Measurement Myopia*. Retrieved July 10, 2017, from http://www.druckerinstitute.com/2013/07/measurement-myopia/

5. Amy Ann Fortni and Rob van der Meulen, *Gartner's 2016 Hype Cycle for Emerging Technologies Identifies Three Trends That Organizations Must Track to Gain Competitive Advantage*. Retrieved July 10, 2017, from http://www.gartner.com/newsroom/id/3412017

6. Peter Smith (2008), *The Quiet Crisis: How Higher Education Is Failing America* (San Francisco, CA: Jossey-Bass), 94.

7. Randall Bass (2012), *Disrupting Ourselves: The Problem of Learning in Higher Education*. Retrieved July 10, 2017, from http://er.educause.edu/articles/2012/3/disrupting-ourselves-the-problem-of-learning-in-higher-education

8. Joanne Cleaver (2012), *The Career Lattice: Combat Brain Drain, Improve Company Culture, and Attract Top Talent* (New York: McGraw-Hill).

9. Bureau of Labor Statistics (2017), *Number of Jobs Held in a Lifetime*. Retrieved July 10, 2017, from https://www.bls.gov/nls/nlsfaqs.htm#anch41

10. Patricia Cranton (1994), *Understanding and Promoting Transformative Learning: A Guide for Educators of Adults* (New York: John Wiley & Sons).

11. Joann Horton (2015), "Identifying At-Risk Factors That Affect College Student Success." *International Journal of Process Education* 7, no. 1. Available at http://www.processeducation.org/ijpe/2015/risk.pdf

12. Pete McDonnell, ed. (2016), *The Experiential Library: Transforming Academic and Research Libraries through the Power of Experiential Library* (Cambridge, UK: Chandros Publishing).

13. Online Learning Consortium (2015), *2015 Online Report Card: Tracking Online Education in the United States*. Available at https://onlinelearningconsortium.org/read/online-report-card-tracking-online-education-united-states-2015/. Also useful are https://www.nmc.org/pdf/Future-of-Higher-Ed-(NMC).pdf, and https://campustechnology.com/articles/2016/03/14/7-things-higher-educati on-innovators-want-you-to-know.aspx

SIX
Program and Course Design for the New Majority

William A. Egan

With the rise of New Majority students and advances in educational technology, institutions are transitioning to new delivery models and formats. These initiatives have the promise to improve an institution's positioning within the competitive landscape of higher education. The goal is to find the right balance of demand, cost, and quality while being able to align with institutional goals and objectives.

Tying strategic decisions to this framework provides a perspective from which to identify and match the resources required to implement new programs and services targeted to serve New Majority students. Instructional designers can provide value throughout the implementation through their essential insight into teaching, learning, and student-support approaches that are mission-centered and sustainable.

Instructional designers have experience leading the design and development of online and hybrid courses that connect to New Majority learners across the world. Instructional designers offer a unique perspective when it comes to the planning, design, and implementation of academic programs and courses. They have an innate ability to think systematically and step back to see the "big picture," while at the same time being able to easily shift thinking to understand how the granular elements of a single course, lesson, module, activity, or assessment fit within that "big picture." With a unique position—situated among the administration, faculty, and student dynamic—they can see how one decision can impact the rest of the system. It is part of the instructional designer's role to help identify these impacts and provide consultation for consideration when necessary.

When choosing to implement and deliver new instructional models or formats, it is important to recognize that any redesign occurs at both the program and course level. All decisions related to program redesign directly impact the necessary course redesign, and then ultimately, impact student-learning outcomes as well as their satisfaction and disposition to reenroll. A ripple effect can be seen throughout the system.

Effective designs align with the institution's mission and goals, with priorities for resource allocations and enrollment targets, with faculty members' quality commitment and workload expectations, and with students' learning and career goals. Stakeholders' access and engagement expectations are the foundation of a virtuous cycle of growth, reinvestment, and renewal. Ineffective designs, on the other hand, do not work because they fail to attend to the needs of their multiple constituents: administrators who focus on sustaining the institution, faculty who focus on sustaining the field, and learners who will vote with their feet if the learning environment is isolating or unmanageable given the complexities of their lives and their skills in technology, self-direction, and help-seeking.

Terminology is an important consideration when distinguishing between program- and course-level redesign. For example, the Online Learning Consortium (OLC) offers a definition of a blended *course*, which would consist of a mixture of online and face-to-face instructional activity. On the other hand, a blended *program* is defined as offering students a combination of traditional face-to-face courses with fully online courses for program completion. Without the clear distinction between the *course* and *program* levels, miscommunication and misunderstandings are bound to arise. Ensure that any terminology used is clearly defined and established early within any process to adopt new instructional models or formats.

PROGRAM DESIGN CONSIDERATIONS

With many possibilities for program formats, along with new and creative solutions being constantly explored, it is important to evaluate each option for how it aligns with institutional priorities. The format chosen has impacts on both cost and learning. Cost includes not only expenditures for the technology and the designers, but format will also impact faculty workload, including reassigned time or stipends for course development, piloting, assessment, and continuous improvement.

There are also costs for students in terms of time, energy, and the expenses associated with coming to campus, buying course materials, and paying fees for technology access. The degree to which a format promotes students' abilities to learn from and with others and to demonstrate relevant, authentic learning is key to the choice in format.

As an example, consider a program designed specifically for students of the New Majority. Flexibility and convenience are a few of the most-cited needs when it comes to nontraditional and adult learners, but these are also qualities that are valued by Gen Z learners who have been raised to value practical, independent, and accessible learning at any time from any device within the world of the Internet of Things (IOT). A traditional, face-to-face, campus-based program centered on individual courses offered for three hours a week may be neither convenient for a New Majority learner nor palatable for a Gen Z.

Administrators and faculty should work with instructional designers to share their knowledge of their current students and their awareness of emerging needs among demographic bands targeted for institutional growth.

In the same vein, hybrid designs have promise to offer enhanced pedagogy, increased access and flexibility, and improved cost effectiveness[1] and can lead to unique teaching strategies that are not found exclusively in face-to-face or online learning environments. At a program level, hybrid courses can be coordinated so students can take two courses in the face-to-face time of one.

Hybrid courses can appeal to a variety of student-learning styles and offer a flexible means of communication, collaboration, and assessment.[2] For New Majority students who may have been away from education for a time, a hybrid course can serve to transition naturally from everyday life to academics.[3]

Although it's tempting to see hybrid formats as the "best of both worlds," institutional goals and culture, faculty concerns and constraints, facility demands, and students' access expectations can also make hybrid courses the worst of both worlds. If the face-to-face and online portions of a hybrid program are not intentionally designed to take advantage of the benefits of each milieu, the learning environment can be taxing, befuddling, and ineffectual.

Fully online programs depend on learners to be disciplined, self-directing, highly literate and able to consume and manage information that comes from texts and from multimedia. The learners must have reliable access to Internet technologies and must know enough about the college and program to identify support resources when needed. Faculty must learn and adapt pedagogies of engagement to the online environment and must consider the security of testing and the authenticity of student work. The institution must give care to accreditation issues, cyber security, and a range of student services, including access to the library, online payment, and even counseling and advising services.

At the program level, crucial decisions and expectations need to be established to ensure a quality learning experience is delivered to students. The goal of administration is to find a balance between cost and quality of learning within the confines of institutional mission, so the first step of program-level redesign is to assess the needs and goals of stakeholders, including administrators, faculty, students, accrediting organizations, and the wider college community. Additionally, instructional design and instructional technologists should also be included in planning for the potential impact on the individual course-design process within the program-level decision making. These are only a few examples of potential stakeholders; but given the costs and the stakes of success, it is wise to err on the side of inclusion.

With the stakeholders and their goals and needs known, focus then needs to be placed on clarifying intended outcomes. This includes establishing consistent terminology and understanding of any formats being considered. This is the opportunity to ensure all stakeholders are on the same page. For example, it may be possible for online courses in the program to consist of synchronous online webinar sessions. Is the course still considered an "online" course? Some may consider this hybrid because of the synchronous nature of the online webinar sessions. So, which is it?

Answering these questions is necessary for institutional effectiveness, financial aid, and enrollment management staff to do their work regarding accreditation, external reporting, student advising and matriculation processes, marketing, and outreach. All students in general, and New Majority students in particular, need clear, concrete, and concise information about the learning environment, including the demands on their time, the required level of technical expertise, and how they will benefit from the mode of access and from the transferable learning and technical skills presented in the learning environment.

Terminology and methods of delivery may differ across higher education, but the minimal goal should be to establish consistency across each individual institution. In establishing consistent expectations for the program, start with the accrediting bodies to examine how they define and interpret learning formats, and they can help provide additional oversight in the implementation process along with the potential of saving time in the accreditation-review process.

In clarifying outcomes (at the institutional, program, course, and enrollment management levels), additional expectations and program-wide details will come into focus. For example, enrollment numbers and caps on the number of students in a particular course or program may have significant impact on the format chosen because they impact revenue, resources, faculty workload, and instructional design. Think of it in terms of a traditional classroom. Direct instruction varies in a small class of fifteen students compared to large lecture hall of more than a hundred students. The same applies to online, hybrid, or any other alternative format. Setting enrollment figures and communicating these expectations to all stakeholders can help to avoid costs associated with necessary course revisions in the event enrollment caps change in the future.

A comprehensive inventory of existing resources and infrastructure can help reduce costs and streamline the process of adopting new instructional models. For instance, institutions may have an existing network of satellite campuses and locations, and individual or clusters of sites may align with the program's targeted demographic for expanding enrollment. Program and course designs that serve those students' needs while scaling institutional investments can be strategically leveraged and lead to an opportunity for synchronous distributed courses.

Other program-level administrative decisions include course sequencing within the program and aligning program outcomes with industry or accreditation standards or with the institution's graduation goals. The design will affect the data available on student progress and learning and the ease of access to this data for faculty and administration to consider.

Technology can be a significant investment when transitioning the delivery of a program. Rather than immediately determining that new technologies are needed, existing resources may be adapted to online, hybrid, or other formats of instruction or to connect physical campus locations for synchronous distributed instruction. Web-conferencing tools may be in place to help students connect remotely or multimedia labs available to help faculty produce their own video. New delivery models or strategies may very well emerge based on the creative use of the existing technology infrastructure.

People within the institution and the expertise that they provide are other essential resources. Multimedia staff can assist faculty in producing engaging video to use for online instruction. Student services staff may be experts in ensuring accessibility of instructional content across multiple learning environments. Instructional technology staff can assist with leveraging the learning management system and available tools to enhance instruction.

Regardless of the learning environment, instructional designers can be essential to working with faculty to rethink and adapt instruction to new formats. Instructional design resources can provide the most impact during the course-design process, but by involving instructional design early during administration's program planning phase, their expertise can help create a strategic path for implementation.

COURSE-DESIGN ROLES

Once the redesign shifts to the course level, roles of the original stakeholders involved can begin to change. Depending on resources available, the key players in the course-redesign process may differ. There are two common approaches to course design, having the faculty lead the process or having instructional designers lead. Either approach can be successful, and the institution's choice will center largely on staff and faculty strengths and existing governance processes.

Faculty-led approaches often rely on the availability of faculty members who are highly skilled at aligning technologies with teaching and learning goals and who have a strong voice for academic quality standards. Having these attributes eases both the technology-centered decisions and curriculum/program approval discussions. Ideally the faculty leader will work in close partnership with an instructional designer.

If instructional design services are unavailable, the faculty would serve as both the instructional designer and the subject matter expert (SME). Faculty development resources may be required to adequately prepare faculty to undertake the demands of course development independently. In a faculty-led approach, it is recommended that the course is not designed in a silo. If possible, have multiple faculty members coauthor or codesign a course. Having colleagues and peers to help brainstorm, plan, and rethink instruction can lead to dynamic discussions and creative ideas around redesigning courses for a new format.

In an instructional design–led approach, the faculty can focus on the content and expertise they bring to the course, and the instructional designer interprets this foundation to create an approach that connects program and course learning outcomes to institutional goals and to necessary technologies.

In collaboration with all stakeholders, an instructional designer refines the design to the pilot stage and helps to analyze data and feedback from the pilot to refine processes and resources for full implementation. In either model, the value of instructional design resources during development phases can be essential to creating a quality learning experience for students.

Instructional designers can potentially serve many functions throughout the design of a course. Project manager, trainer, instructional technologist, accessibility consultant, graphic designer, copyright specialist, programmer, and so on are only a handful of possible responsibilities or skills of an instructional designer. Through their project-management acumen, an instructional designer can coordinate all available resources to ensure a course is completed on time and on budget. If an institution has access to multimedia, accessibility, copyright, or educational technology specialists, the designer can strategically bring this group together to manage specific tasks, which allows the instructional designer to have even more time to focus on adapting the instruction with the faculty.

Administration and lead faculty still play a role in the course-design process in the instructional design–led approach. Because it is quite rare for instructional designers to have any direct authority over faculty or SMEs, the instructional designer and administration need to work together to create a level of accountability to ensure that development milestones are completed on time and any deadlines along the way are met, all while preserving the valuable working relationship between the designer and faculty. It can be quite a balancing act. Administration or a designated lead faculty member can also provide checks and balances along the way by reviewing course outlines, syllabi, and lessons to ensure standards are being met.

PRINCIPLES OF COURSE DESIGN FOR THE NEW MAJORITY

New Majority learners have been characterized in this book as being students whose preparation for higher education has been substantially different from the standard on which many college programs are based. As depicted by Sereni in chapter 2 and by Weber in chapter 4, New Majority learners have likely entered our institutions through one or more of these circumstances:

1. Because of family or other environmental conditions, students never imagined they would have access to college right after high school, so they didn't acquire a broad scope of understanding of college-going processes and decisions and have likely chosen an institution based first on economic factors or convenience so they can continue to work while in school. Therefore, even though they may not have the outward appearance of New Majority learners, they may have some need for clear explanations and effective transition experiences to help them to feel a sense of fit with the institution.
2. They delayed entering higher education directly after high school and acquired not only substantial work and life experiences but also substantial competing responsibilities and priorities. As with the first category, they often center their choice of program on access and career benefit, but they also value connection to other older students. They may need to develop or adapt technology skills and to have meaningful and individualized ways to connect to their advisors, faculty members, and peers.
3. They stopped out of higher education at least once and often many times. The stop-out choice may have been centered on academic challenges, personal conflicts, gaps in financial resources, or even the opportunity to seize a valuable alternative experience. In any case, they are wary "shoppers" and are looking with scrutiny to the on-boarding processes (financial aid, advising, registration, orientation) and to the quality of the learning experience, and they too want access and ease in managing multiple responsibilities.

All these perspectives will impact choices while redesigning and developing courses. It can be easy to become overwhelmed, so don't be afraid to step back and revisit the basics of course design throughout the development process to maintain focus. Outlined are a few principles and best practices to help jump-start a foundation for quality course design. By no means is this a complete list, so development lists should be tailored to meet the specific needs of the institution.

Manage Time

Time can both be a friend and an enemy during the course-design process. It all depends on how the course-development timeline and associated milestones are managed. Ideally, the earlier that development can start, the better to account for any unplanned disruptions along the way. With a realistic understanding of the commitment needed during development, team members can be prepared to allocate sufficient time to the course-development process, adapt timelines as necessary, and stay motivated throughout the process.

Align Learning Objectives

The foundation of any good instruction and course design begins with the learning objectives. Regardless of format, the alignment of measurable course and lesson learning objectives with accessible and relevant assessments ensures that a course's quality and effectiveness can be evaluated, and improvements can be implemented without wholesale continuous redesign.

Value the Student Perspective

Pull from the previous experiences of faculty as they learned new technology skills. If they have taught a hybrid or online course, how did they learn to do so? What were the resources and messages that helped them to be successful? Many faculty members have also taken hybrid or online courses as adults. What worked to make them feel engaged and connected to their peers? What didn't work? These reflections can help faculty think from the perspective of the New Majority and assist in forming the vision for what the course should be.

Furthermore, don't forget about the students as stakeholders. Be sure to bring students in at various stages of the design process and ensure that there are channels built into the pilot for them to provide feedback to help drive the direction of refinement processes. A student-centered approach means you don't automatically substitute your judgment for their lived experiences. Give the highest priority to design elements that help students with access and that eliminate barriers to their success.

Be Flexible and Adapt

Faculty should not feel like they are limited by the development process. Just like students have flexibility, instructors and faculty have flexibility while teaching. Student interest, current events, or online discussions may take the course in a different direction. Instructors are encouraged to customize their teaching based on the specific needs of the students in their class and find ways to ensure the faculty "voice" is heard throughout the course. For instance, in an asynchronous online course, relevant current events and work experiences that may help students make connections to the content can be easily shared via announcements, class e-mails, or in designated content pages and discussions.

Rethink Lectures

From an instructional design perspective, one of the biggest challenges when working with faculty who are new to adapting instruction for alternative formats such as online and hybrid, is to remove themselves from the traditional lecture mind-set. Posting static PowerPoint slides, embedding voice-over hour-long PowerPoint lecture videos, or broadcasting videos of live lecture hall class sessions no longer meet quality standards for distance education.

Faculty should be empowered to rethink their teaching and step outside of the lecture mind-set to deliver quality instruction for new learning formats. In chapter 5, Walsh provides some excellent suggestions for tools and strategies to explore, and instructional designers can help with this shift in thinking. In keeping with the call to be adaptable and flexible, remember that integrated technology should add value to student learning and not become a barrier to learning. Leverage the tools and structure of a learning management system to organize the components of the online course and to facilitate any online collaboration.

Remember Orientation

At the start of the course or cohort, dedicate a time for orientation to properly introduce the learning environment and course structure. Communicate clear course expectations, policies, and provide students with tips for success to help them transition into a new learning environment. Use the orientation to introduce any technology used in the course and to provide opportunity for practice to ensure there are no technology-related issues later. This is also a great chance to form a community among students and build a connection to the program, department, and institution. Having strong connections and developing a feeling of learning in community can help in motivating students and could lead to higher retention rates.

Communicate

Just as communication is essential throughout the design process, it is crucial during implementation. Use the learning management system and any online component to explicitly outline all instructions and expectations on a consistent basis. Use course e-mail, in-course chat or text functions, or announcement tools for posting reminders or added direction. Be available to students both online and in person. If students are in a common geographical region, try to hold office hours both on campus and online to be more accessible to students. Some online faculty even keep "office hours" at a local coffee shop or public library to ensure that students can get the individualized and responsive support they need to persist.

New Majority students may complete most of their work over the weekends because of various obligations. Be sure to provide contact information for any technical support resources that may be available to students during traditional and nontraditional hours as well.

Provide Structure and Sequence

Avoid using the learning management system as a file repository. Do not simply use the system to arbitrarily post files and areas to submit assignments without context. Provide students structure and clear direction. For example, include lesson introductions with the stated learning objectives, lesson content and commentary, and lesson summaries with an outline of activities and assignment expectations. Any expertise in usability, including test runs with students, can help create an easily navigable and cohesive course environment for students.

Multimedia

Be cautious of how multimedia, graphics, and video content are integrated. Be mindful of multimedia best practices such as copyright, viewer attention span, and audio and video quality. If video content or graphics don't add value to the lesson and support the learning objectives, written commentary may be just as effective. Multimedia is a great way to appeal to multiple learning styles and can be valuable for engagement when used properly, but be cautious because it can be a distraction to learning if not used properly.

Accessibility

Accessibility should always be considered in any learning environment, especially when there is a robust online component to the course. Ensure online content, multimedia, and learning activities meet accessibility standards for students who may have accommodations to disclose.

For example, transcripts and captions for audio and video content as well as alternative text descriptions for images and tables that are embedded within content pages should all be addressed. Use a screen reader to properly test and check that accessibility standards are being met.

Evaluation

A redesigned or new course is never perfect in its first rendition after development. It may take several offerings of a course to get it to the level of quality that it needs to be. Develop a process or use an instrument, such as the Quality Matters rubric, for evaluating the quality of the course. Establish ways to collect student feedback on the course design and structure of the course. Have faculty reflect on their teaching experience and identify areas of improvement to the content and overall design. Take an iterative approach to design by having a formal evaluation process, where resources can be efficiently allocated to plan strategic revisions of courses and maintain quality.

Course-Redesign Examples

Instructional designers love sharing course-design "war stories," celebrating their successes and learning new strategies and approaches based on the challenges of others. It is valuable to pick the brain of an instructional designer to learn even more from their experiences in the course-development trenches. Here are some success stories to share.

Critical Thinking with Scenarios

In an online nursing program made up of primarily working adults in the profession, the goal is to expand on the RN competencies with a focus on advanced critical thinking and leadership to help students progress in their careers. The design team turned to developing interactive decision-based scenarios where background information was provided for a specific case, and students are faced with decision points and presented with options based on possible outcomes.

Consequences are then provided to students based on their selection, and they continue through the scenario down a "path" where they may stumble along the way or find themselves to a successful end. This approach allows students to practice critical thinking in a safe environment. It also exposes students to new situations that they may not have experience with in their area of nursing. Students can then reflect on their experience with the decision-based scenarios, identify areas for remediation if necessary, and prepare to apply concepts in an authentic clinical environment of their own.

Introductions and Icebreakers

Sometimes it is the little things in the course design that can make a big impact in the overall experience of students. During a course revision for an online graduate-level engineering course, the design team wanted to include a stronger faculty presence or voice within the course and forge a stronger connection to students at a distance and decided to create short icebreaker videos for each lesson to be embedded on the lesson introduction pages. Each lesson's introduction page includes a brief written lesson overview, lesson learning objectives, and a fun video clip to get students interested and excited about the lesson.

The video clips were intended to be a fun way to connect students to the faculty. Videos were often spoofs of classic TV shows or late night talk show bits with the lesson's themes intertwined. The videos were short 3- to 5-minute clips with transcripts and captioning to stay in alignment with multimedia and accessibility best practices. They also supported the overall course by introducing each lesson in an engaging manner. In their feedback, students enjoyed seeing their instructors in an informal context and looked forward to a new video each week.

CONCLUSION

As educational technology and instructional design evolve, so will the instructional models and delivery formats that are used across higher education. Regardless of new technology and trends, the foundation of every course is good pedagogy and design. Bad pedagogy is bad pedagogy, regardless of the teaching environment or format, so by ensuring quality design and teaching standards are met, a successful learning experience can be established to serve the students of the New Majority and beyond.

By recognizing the need for a redesign from the top down, institutions can strategically position themselves to offer quality and cost-effective education for students in the New Majority. Take advantage of valuable instructional-design resources to make implementation manageable for stakeholders while also being able to provide faculty with the consultation and confidence needed to adapt their teaching for delivery in new formats. Challenges may be encountered and difficult decisions may have to be made throughout the redesign of programs and courses, but as long as the impact on student learning drives the process and decisions being made, institutions can position themselves to continue to offer competitive educational opportunities for students in the New Majority.

NOTES

1. Charles R. Graham, Stephanie Allen, and Donna Ure (2005), "Benefits and challenges of blended learning environments," in *Encyclopedia of Information Science and Technology* (Hershey, PA: IRMA), 253–259.

2. Roberta Gogos (2014), "Why Blended Learning Is Better." Retrieved July 11, 2017, from https://elearningindustry.com/why-blended-learning-is-better

3. Jordan Friedman (2015), "Decide Between Online, Blended Courses." *U.S. News & World Report*. Retrieved July 10, 2016, from http://www.usnews.com/education/online-education/articles/2015/03/04/decide-between-online-blended-courses

SEVEN

The Financial Dimension: Institutional Readiness for New Majority Learners

Eric Malm and Marguerite Weber

Throughout this book, several authors have recognized the value of the New Majority learners as a catalyst for academic transformation. New Majority learners will, of necessity, change our institutions.

First, their growing numbers, matched with a shrinking demographic of seventeen to twenty-one-year-old students who are being financially supported will change recruitment, matriculation, transition, teaching, retention, and graduation policies, processes, and systems. And too, competitors are scrambling for students' attention through online courses, badges, and for-profits schools. Drawn to more agile and responsive peer institutions or for-profit start-ups, the New Majority students in our catchment areas will vote with their feet when they see possibilities that are better fits for their access issues, that provide appropriate supports, and that promise a good value for their time and financial investments.

Second, especially at institutions with access missions, the New Majority learner will help us to refine our practices and pedagogies of engagement. Typically vocal about needs, active in seeking out services, and generous with describing their experiences, New Majority learners provide those of us open to listening to, learning from, and ultimately acting on what students tell us with crucial insights into the student experience for all learners. When we hear them better, institutions will align academic transformation efforts with the social justice of conforming what we do to serve those to whom we've opened our doors.

Finally, as seen especially in the chapters by Walsh and Egan, emerging technologies and emerging industries will change our practice and focus to prepare our students with emerging literacies that make our students competitive in the global economy, responsive in our diverse communities, and agile in the gig employment culture.

But who is going to pay for this transformation?

This chapter examines economic issues facing institutions and students. Because the intention of this work is to provide perspectives across institutional constituents, here we include a primer that pulls back the curtain on the basics of college budgeting. Those who are considering academic transformation to serve New Majority learners will need to understand how to frame budgeting conversations to do more, or to do differently in a cash-strapped do-more-with-less current economic environment for higher education.

Then there are cost-benefit examples of academic innovations that fit New Majority learners' needs at scalable cost-value propositions. Those skilled in designing and delivering programs and services for New Majority learners have an advocacy role and a social justice imperative. Scholars and practitioners across higher education have much to learn from New Majority–serving professionals, as arguably, wholesale changes in approaches to teaching and learning will be necessary to sustain fragile individual institutions and higher education as a larger construct.

Lastly, we look at the cost-value propositions from the students' perspectives, as those who are increasing their institutional readiness for New Majority learners will need new ways to talk about going to college. Moreover, value propositions are impacted by wasteful barriers to student success and progress, and students need the skills to navigate those impediments and institutions need the vision to eliminate them. In an atmosphere of competition for students' time, attention, and goodwill, articulating the value of higher education is more important than ever.

BUDGETING IN HIGHER EDUCATION

In top-down budgets, operating units and departments are expected to operate within budgets that are designated by the administration. For example, in performance-responsibility budgeting,[1] operating units are given budgets based on past performance and expected future need.

Therefore, if a department's enrollment is expected to grow (or drop), or there is some anticipated increase (or decrease) in costs, administration can take this into account and raise (or lower) the budget. In tight times, across-the-board budget freezes can be implemented in the hopes that individual departments will be able to best determine where funding cuts would be least painful. In times of plenty, budgets can be increased at a common rate with possible adjustments based on perceived need.

Top-down budgeting approaches are used in many institutions[2] and for a clear reason—for many years they have worked. In a relatively stable academic atmosphere, budgets that meet student needs in one year are likely to meet student needs in the following year, and the administration can make adjustments with feedback from people within operating units (such as departments or schools) to make arguments for increased funding based on enrollment.

But, in rapidly changing times, these top-down approaches may not work well and may actually impede progress. When budgets are based on what a department did the previous year, the safest approach, arguably, is to continue past practices. Adding a new budget category may be difficult and may risk the continuation of a "tried-and-true" practice. Top-down approaches would be expected to encourage the continuation of traditional teaching approaches and discourage alternative approaches, especially if these new approaches required either new or different expenditures.[3]

Top-down approaches may also have unintended consequences regarding spending on university-wide support resources. For example, administration may invest in computer hardware, software, and support to be used across the university. Once these resources are in place and staffed, change becomes more difficult and the perpetuation of the basic technology model becomes embedded in the budgeting structure.

As a common resource, no individual department will likely want to have sole responsibility to pay for upgrades, the benefits of which are shared with other departments. If central administration is not able to see the full value of the resource, economic theory suggests that underinvestment in the shared resource will result.[4]

Other approaches take measures of revenue and performance into consideration. In the responsibility-center budgeting[5] approach, departments or schools receive budgets equal to the revenue they generate. Although this approach places a strong revenue-generating focus on operating units, it may cause inappropriate competition between departments (for example, a business school may discourage students from taking courses in the English department). This approach is also complicated by the fact that most students enroll in a college to take advantage of a variety of programs and attributes, whose value may not be easily identified or separated by administration.

A particular challenge to activities-based budgeting, and indeed to any kind of enrollment-driven formula, is that of shared costs. Universities have an enormous number of shared costs, from buildings and grounds to the library to academic support services and residence life staff. Additional students or a new program may place added burdens, for example, on the library.[6] Additional book titles or online subscriptions may need to be purchased, and the demand for library resources may expand. In the zero-sum game of university budgeting, departments may be seen as competing for resources specific to their programming but are unlikely to want to contribute toward (or be billed) for the use or expansion of shared resources.

THE AFFORDABILITY CHALLENGE

Although all colleges and universities have learning at the center of their mission, no institution can be successful without a strong financial base. As practitioners strive to redesign courses and programs, they must also do so with the bottom line in mind. Old ways of budgeting may actually stifle innovation. And if new programs and approaches are all "additive," there is the real prospect of cost bloat. Thus, the challenge is to find ways to cater to a growing student population in ways that is affordable to the student and sustainable to the institution.

In short, as discussed in the Griffin chapter, adult learning programs are often seen as fund-positive with not much additional spending needed. If a school can recruit adults to take up seats that are emptied from declining enrollments (due to declining demographics for traditionally aged students), then why should there be additional expenses for anything other than recruiting and marketing dollars?

As this volume has demonstrated, New Majority learners need a well-crafted and supportive student experience. Given the funding conundrum described here, effective administrators will develop strategies and systems to capture the return on investment (ROI) for these individualizing initiatives. That is, serving New Majority learners can be a mission-driven imperative, but without generating income, the mission of the entire institution is jeopardized.

Here's a way to think about the work. Start with a cost-learning depiction, following Rubin's categorization of "craft" and "mass production" models of higher education.[7] Figure 7.1 allows for plotting institutions or programs along cost and learning dimensions. A well-funded, highly selective college with an 8:1 student-to-faculty ratio, for example, could represent the craft model. In such an institution, with excellent facilities and abundant personal attention, one expects that significant learning will take place but at a high cost.

In contrast, Rubin's "mass production" model describes many for-profit institutions that deliver relatively low-cost online education to large numbers of students. In these largely online, for-profit universities, adjunct instructors typically deliver predefined courses to large numbers of students; if one takes retention and graduation rates as proxies for learning, these institutions deliver significantly less learning per student, for significantly less cost.

The craft model is depicted as conveying high levels of learning at high costs. The mass production model portrays lower levels of learning at lower costs. Within this context, a question emerges as to whether it is possible to restructure courses or programs to deliver higher levels of learning at a lower cost.

A challenge for both mass production and craft institutions is whether there are ways to improve the cost effectiveness of learning, reducing the cost of learning for craft institutions, or increasing the amount of learning for mass production institutions. As we search for structures that allow for optimal learning and affordability, this cost-of-learning framework encourages stakeholders to explicitly think about the trade-offs between cost and the amount of learning.

Implicit in this framework are the ideas that costs do matter and that costs and formats do affect student learning. For administrators, faculty, and program designers, this framework pushes an explicit discussion of more cost-effective (although not necessarily lower cost) ways of structuring courses and programs. It should be noted that restructuring when, where, and how learning takes place often means replacing some resources with others (like replacing classrooms with online space or leveraging on-campus writing support services, for example). So, within this context it is important to discuss the important role of shared resources.

By connecting an activities-based budget to a deep understanding of shared costs, program designers and the administrators who support them can demonstrate the agility and entrepreneurship at the foundation of truly responsive New Majority–focused programs. That is, by connect-

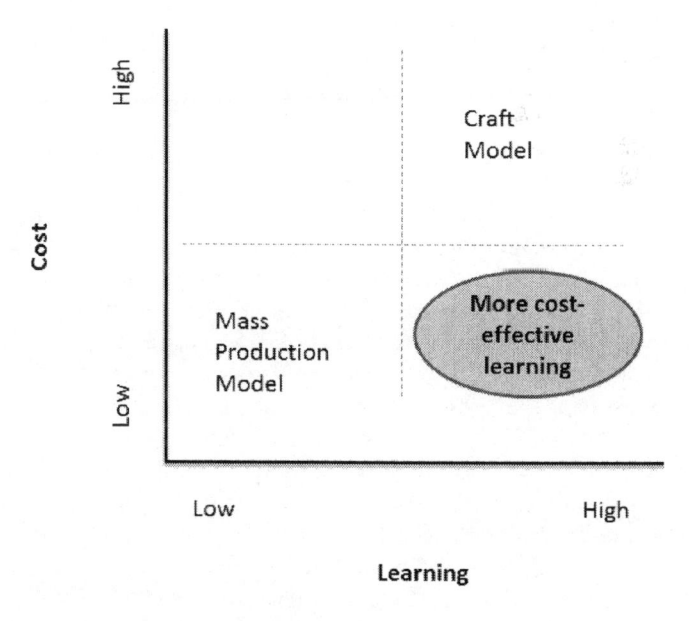

Figure 7.1. The cost of learning framework

ing these kinds of programs and services to the institution's access and social justice missions and by determining the degree to which academic transformation for New Majority learners can be a catalyst to wider changes that bring about improvements in efficiency and effectiveness.

In the approaches explored, what's needed is the trust between the program designer and the chief financial officer to be able to say, "For every $2 you give me today, I will return $3 as soon as the program reaches maturity. And you'll keep earning that extra $1.00 not only on my program but in other programs as they adapt redesign strategies that are appropriate to their work." A year-to-year balanced budget cycle can test the mettle of that trust bond.

As various chapters in this book have demonstrated, building truly responsive learning programs and services for New Majority learners takes innovation and individualization, and those processes take funding. However, if program designers start with an eye toward innovation rather than recreating traditional learning environments with traditional cost structures, New Majority programs can be developed to be self-sustaining and, when the innovations are scaled across the campus, they can help to both lower the college's overall costs and increase student persistence.

REDESIGN PROCESSES

Carol Twigg,[8] an early pioneer of course redesign, led a national movement to reimagine the classroom, especially for high-enrollment introductory courses. The National Center for Academic Transformation (NCAT), which Twigg founded, supported course redesign initiatives in more than thirty states.

The essential quality-improvement strategies that are common to course-redesign principles are continuous access to online tutorial materials, instant assessment and feedback, increased interaction among students, on-demand support in multiple modes (online, face-to-face, small group, etc.), and flexibility with time on task (mastery learning to scheduled milestones). The results were consistent: quality was enhanced, retention was improved, access was expanded, and capacity was increased.

The "mantra" of the NCAT movement focuses on cost containment: either expand capacity while maintaining student success outcomes and costs (thus reducing the cost per student) or maintain capacity and outcomes while lowering overall program cost. Indeed, many redesign initiatives, especially those focused on reimagining developmental/remedial studies have been able to accomplish both.

For example, in a redesign project at an urban public university, Weber[9] developed a model for developmental math courses that increased capacity by more than 30 percent, lowered costs by 13 percent, and increased first-time pass rates by more than 20 percent. The model was a New Majority–appropriate reimagination of the emporium model, allowing students to choose not only whether they wanted to learn in a classroom or in a coached lab environment but also to choose which class and which frequency of attending proved the best fit for their needs. With choice of learning mode and frequency, the learning expanded to include students' developing an understanding of work processes that yield good solutions.

The academic transformation movement started with a focus on "gateway" courses, those large, lecture-style classrooms that new students needed to learn to navigate before they can get to more individualized learning experiences that were awaiting them if they could just get to the upper division. Then the movement expanded to the problem of remediation. High-placement rates coupled with low-course pass rates formed a near impenetrable barrier to on-time graduation.

Then, other practitioners started to apply the findings to wholesale institutional redesign.[10] The resulting trend toward analyzing student persistence behaviors through the lens-of-choice architecture has created many reimagined approaches to serving students, including meta-majors, guided pathways, and advising redesign.[11] New Majority–learning program designers can and should incorporate these hard-won gains in higher education cost-containment and ROI strategies from the inception of a new program.

An example is in order. In chapter 4, Weber presents the Access Pedagogy model as an adapted high-impact practice (HIP) for adult learning. The approach is high impact because it promotes deep learning through active and collaborative experiences where students practice diffused leadership in a variety of settings. It promotes student success because the instructional "labor" is dispersed to all of the members of the learning environment: the student takes responsibility for acquiring content through the online environment, and the learning mentor runs the "face-to-face" time and facilitates students' learning using the content across the boundaries of paired courses.

The shared labor of students and mentor afford space and time for the faculty members from each of the paired courses space to provide higher-quality interactions—those focused on how experts use the subject, what they find beautiful and useful in this way of seeing the world, and how students can be engaged as potential future colleagues who also celebrate and refine this disciplinary knowledge.

But this model also aligns with the NCAT cost-containment philosophy: improve outcomes, expand capacity, increase access, lower costs. Here's how: The Access Pedagogy model starts with the principle that the highest-cost item in the budget should go to the highest-value ROI. A college course delivers three returns on the members' contribution of time, energy, and goodwill.

1. Students acquire new content.
2. Students develop the habits of mind and the habits of collaboration to practice the essential processes of the discipline.
3. Students develop a personal interest in and commitment to the value of the discipline, learning to appreciate how the discipline communicates and solves problems.

In a traditional classroom, the faculty member is responsible for creating the learning environment, for providing substantive formative and summative feedback on students' mastery of content, for coaching students on their abilities to exercise proper habits valued by the discipline, and for engaging learners as potential colleagues and capturing their imagination on what value students can add to the discipline's essential premises and what unanswered questions are left to explore. Fill up the class with at least the twenty-five to thirty students needed to make the course cost effective, and that's quite a bit on one person's plate.

In the Access Pedagogy, however, there are other adults, none of whom "cost" as much as the faculty member: coaches, mentors, student-development professionals, and even more capable, self-directed students, who can support taking the professor's work to scale.

Technology can also make increasing class size both manageable and learning centered. Identifying smart uses of appropriate technologies can not only increase the learning to include content mastery as well as the work habits of learned people but can improve the economics of the effort, the "business case" for the endeavor.

Here is the hypothetical case that informs the illustration. Let's assume that the faculty member makes $80,000 per year and is responsible for teaching six classes a year, and for scholarly productivity and college service. For argument's sake, then, let's divide the $80,000/year by 8 (6 classes + scholarship + service): $10,000 per class.

Let's also add that the course in question is highly engaging, enriched by the HIP quality dimensions described in chapter 4: frequent, timely, and constructive feedback with structured opportunities to reflect on and integrate learning, investment of time and effort by students over an extended period of time, interactions with faculty and peers about substantive matters, and opportunities to discover the relevance of learning through real-world applications.

Because the course offers such an enriching environment, the maximum class size has been set at sixteen. Typically, because scheduling depends on the faculty member's availability, the class only enrolls ten students, but it's a great class that inspires students to persist, so it runs once a year (thus, it "costs" $1,000 per student in instructional costs).

In most college budgeting formulae, the "overhead" (shared costs) for personnel expenses averages at least 50 percent. That is, for everything from the instructor's benefits to the grounds crew that removes the snow from the parking lot, there's an added premium. Therefore, the actual cost of the instruction is closer to $1,500 per student. Let's also assume that the student pays $300 per credit hour, or $900.

Unless many of the college's other courses are large enrollment courses taught by low-cost adjunct faculty (or unless there is an endless cash reserve), this model is unsustainable. But we must realize that those cost-saving models (i.e., auditorium classes and excessive use of adjunct faculty) are also unsustainable in terms of student persistence and completion outcomes or the instructional quality control measures of most accreditation systems.

Table 7.1 shows that the Access Pedagogy course redesign, informed by HIP, can also result in a sustainable budget model.

The thoughtful reader may declare, "Wait, wait. I saw what you did there. You just upped the class to twenty-one students. Not fair!" Yes, fair, and this is why.

Let's start with the assumption that the faculty member still costs $15,000 ($10,000 per course, plus overhead), and then we pay the learning mentor $24 per hour for 8 hours a week for fifteen weeks (3.5 hours in class plus payment for collaborating with faculty and class preparation + overhead on part-time staff is about 8 percent). That makes a total of $16,944 per course. But, because the content delivery is online and the class meets only once a week (facilitated by the mentor, not the instructor) — and this course is paired with another course to boot — face-to-face sections can be scheduled at multiple times and even at multiple locations, ensuring that the course will fill closer to capacity.

The distribution of responsibilities also makes this both possible and appropriate: the student is responsible for content acquisition by interacting and getting instant formative assessment online; the learning mentor is responsible for facilitating an environment where students practice and apply key processes; and the faculty member is responsible for managing the learning environment, for substantive faculty–student interactions, and for summative assessment.

Table 7.1. Cost-revenue worksheet for traditional and Access Pedagogies

Mode	Cost per student	Revenue per student	Enrollment	Cost per class	Revenue per class	Net
Traditional class	$1,500	$900	10	$15,000	$9,000	($6,000)
Access Pedagogy	$1,577	$1,800	21	($15,000 x 2) + $3,110 = $33,110	$18,900 x 2 = $37,800	$4,690

Moreover, the model is both supportable and portable. These face-to-face meetings can be scheduled at off-campus locations, again providing access to more New Majority students. In this way, an institution need not choose between expanding the college's access mission *or* providing an additional revenue stream. It can do both, and do both well.

COLLEGE FINANCE: A STUDENT PERSPECTIVE

From a student perspective, access to higher education without affordability will force both the New Majority students and the institutions who need them into a fool's bargain. Expedient choices will win out to the detriment of all. The student may mistake training for deep, transformative learning. The institution may mistake alternative revenue streams for a budget lifeline that would allow them to resist changing long enough until more traditional students come their way. And, the institution of higher education takes a hit too as we try to articulate our value in a culture that increasingly sees our product as a piece of paper rather than a deeply transforming experience.

Perhaps it is best to argue that for New Majority learners, higher education needs to be a good value. Consider that older New Majority students, many of whom are paying much of their own way through college, will have a very different value proposition from that of traditional students. First, an older learner will have a different cost basis: although typically not encumbered by residence hall and meal plan costs, adult learners are typically paying for a home, transportation, child care, and myriad other costs associated with day-to-day living. Therefore, for a student with a family, cost of attendance is arguably higher than that for a student who is less encumbered.

In addition, the New Majority learner not only tends to be older but also tends to be more part-time, juggling work and school. Therefore, the amount of financial aid they qualify for is less.[12] Finally, New Majority learners, either by virtue of being older or being more part-time, will get less value out of a college degree because they will have fewer years of increased earnings that result from career attainment after degree completion. Table 7.2 examines a simple contrast.

Even if the career opportunity yields the same salary, the value of the adult's degree will be demonstrably less than that of the traditionally aged student.

This simple example explains the urgency adults have to complete quickly and to complete a degree with high value in the career market. Although it's true that many adults return to school to complete something they had previously started or to achieve a personal goal rather than to advance in career, the call for having high-quality, low-cost programs available for adult learners is clear.

Table 7.2. Student education cost per anticipated year of work

Student situation	Years working	Cost of education ($300/ credit hour for 120 credits)	Cost of education per year of work
22-year-old graduates and works until age 68	46	$36,000	$783
42-year-old graduates and works until age 68	26	$36,000	$1,385

This chapter argues that the craft model compared with the mass production model is a false choice. The promise of designing for the New Majority learner is the promise of lowering costs through making classroom walls more porous (i.e., to instructional designers, to technology, to paraprofessionals, etc.) and making high-value programs scalable and portable, able to reach students where they are and to take them where they're going.

Colleges can do much to lower the costs of learning for New Majority students. We can revise transfer policies, expand experiential learning credit award systems, partner with employers and community organizations to develop discount systems, and work with faculty to lower the costs of instructional materials. With innovative approaches to scaling effective practices and with sharing resulting cost savings (via adjusted tuition rates, fee waivers, open access resources, or book scholarships, etc.) between institutions and the New Majority of learners, colleges can do well and do good.

CONCLUSION

How to create the business case for institutions to be college-ready for the New Majority of learners is largely the purpose of a companion book, *Serving the New Majority Student: Working from within to Transform the Institution*. Placing the New Majority within a new market context of options and competitors, the companion book will help teams to come together and assess institutional culture, goals, and priorities. What is intended here is a reminder that all three design elements are important: human effort (what faculty, students, and staff can do, will do, and should do), technology (how technology scales effort and supports what the humans can't, won't or shouldn't do), and the business case (the value of investments of time, energy, good will and money for all involved).

The urgency and resolution of New Majority learners is a great gift to higher education. Their moment, which is this moment, provides us an opportunity to re-imagine, re-think, and re-invent everything to ensure that higher education holds a vibrant, sustainable place in our culture for centuries to come.

NOTES

1. William F. Massey, ed. (1996), *Resource Allocation in Higher Education* (Ann Arbor: University of Michigan Press).
2. Zierdt 2009; Margaret J. Barr and George S. McClellan (2011), *Budgets and Financial Management in Higher Education*, 2nd ed. (Hoboken, NJ: John Wiley & Sons).
3. See Massey, *Resource Allocation in Higher Education*, pp. 53–54, for example.
4. Garret Hardin (1968), "The Tragedy of the Commons," *Science* 162, no. 3859: 1243–1248.
5. John D. Hummell (2012), *Financing Higher Education: Approaches to Funding at Four Year Public Institutions*. Ohio University Center for Higher Education working paper series. Retrieved July 11, 2017, from https://www.ohio.edu/education/centers-and-partnerships/centers/center-for-higher-education/loader.cfm?csModule=security/getfile&PageID=2149085
6. Donna M. Desrochers Steven Hurlburt (2014), *Trends in College Spending 2011–2014: A Delta Data Update*. American Institutes for Research. Retrieved from: http://www.deltacostproject.org/sites/default/files/products/Delta%20Cost_Trends%20College%20Spending%202001-2011_071414_rev.pdf
7. Beth Rubin (2013), "University Business Models and Online Practices: A Third Way." *Online Journal of Distance and Learning Administration* 16, no. 1. Available at http://www.westga.edu/~distance/ojdla/spring161/rubin.html
8. thencat.org
9. Marguerite Weber (2014), "Design for Student Success."
10. Koproske, 2015.
11. Denley et. al., 2013.
12. Federal Student Aid (n.d.), *Staying Eligible*. Retrieved July 11, 2017, from https://studentaid.ed.gov/sa/eligibility/staying-eligible

EIGHT

Learning with Others: Working with Others to Build the New Majority Institution

An Interview with Dr. Eric Malm and Dr. Marguerite Weber

Beverly Schneller

Drs. Malm (EW) and Weber (MW) sat down with Dr. Beverly Schneller (BS) to discuss how they decided to develop the concept of the New Majority Learner, what they want to accomplish by distinguishing this demographic of students, and what they want to accomplish in these books.

Drs. Malm and Weber met at Cabrini University in 2014. Dr. Weber was the vice president for adult programs (she has since moved on to serve as the vice president of student services at a community college in Maryland), and Dr. Malm is an associate professor of business and economics.

When they began their conversations, Malm was the chair of the faculty technology committee, and Weber had been hired from the University of Baltimore to design, implement, and collaborate on sustaining an adult degree-completion (ADC) program for Cabrini University. Cabrini, like many small liberal arts colleges, was looking for ways to diversify its degree programs to attract students and to create alternative revenues and new ways of providing equity and access to higher education for underserved, largely urban populations.

The New Majority became a way to describe those historically excluded from higher education, those who did not realize higher education could benefit them in their lives and work, and those who were in school or returning to school with employment and family factors that had to be reconciled with the traditional liberal arts educational structures and curricula for these students to succeed and to feel confident in their fit with the institution.

BS: *How did you decide you wanted to work together on this project?*

EM: The book project grew out of periodic conversations with Marguerite and from my growing involvement in the degree-completion program. As the program grew, and I saw how different it was in many respects, I realized the institution needed a "user's guide" to help faculty, staff, and administrators better understand the reasoning behind the design. I presented the idea to our provost and sabbatical committee and got approval to work on the project for a sabbatical semester. We chose the topics and authors based on those with whom we have had successful collaborations as educators, as leaders with a broad base of experience from which to draw, and as stakeholders from across the academic enterprise.

In the years before Marguerite's arrival, I had begun to think more about how our business program could better meet the needs of a changing student population. Following a term from the unemployment statistics, I had coined the term *marginally attached students* to refer to students who arrived in college but weren't really sure if they belonged. Whether due to academic preparation, affordability, [and] competing work and life dynamics, many of my entering freshmen seemed to come with a different set of issues and opportunities than I was accustomed. As Marguerite and I talked about adult learners, I realized that many of my traditionally aged current students faced similar challenges.

Our president had suggested that Marguerite meet me because she was working on a project involving technology. I was interested in learning about the new initiative and found that she gave language to things I had already begun to consider. For example, the idea of using stacked credentials as a pathway through college resonated with me.

We kept finding things in common, but coming from two different viewpoints. I enjoyed the creative and entrepreneurial approaches she brought and her own approach as an "intrapreneur" (that is building client relations for entrepreneurship from within) made the collaboration between us easy to form. She provided a structure for what I was seeking to provide for the students who were late teens early twenties. I had a great deal of excitement about how we could meet the needs of these marginally attached students. I was interested, confused, and intrigued about how the ideas might come to being. I recognized she brought experience and background—both real world and academic—and I trusted her to become a stakeholder in the endeavors.

MW: When I went to Cabrini, I made the commitment to find the faculty champions. Eric gave me a lens through which I could plan the models of instruction. He reminded me of the visible and invisible aspects of faculty–administrative collaborations.

I had to learn a new way to operate in patterns that aligned with the differing points of view. For example, when I went out to recruit the community college partners, the administrators there immediately saw the value of having a university partner for an on-site ADC program. The faculty members and some administrators at our own institution, however, took more time to determine if the ADC program was a good fit for Cabrini. Ultimately, we all came to realize we could not work without each other. The program would only succeed if there was a strong partnership, especially with faculty.

EM: Marguerite invited me to help plan the launch of the program. In time, I looked at the first year as the product development year. In my previous business career, I learned not to unveil a new product until it was done. If the sales or operations folks saw a product that was half-baked, internal resistance would grow. And if sales people felt that the new product would be better than what they currently had to offer, they would start selling it even before it was ready to be released.

MW: This was a challenge with the ADC program because the main objective was to get full faculty or broad faculty buy-in. As an example, using the Access Pedagogy meant ceding personal contact to a classroom mentor who was not a subject matter expert. And this was a significant change for most faculty. Moreover, many did not have experience creating collaborative assignments that linked one course to another. In several ways it was a different instructional model.

My experience seemed to echo what had happened when I was a very young junior faculty member at a community college engaged in the assessment-as-learning movement. It took quite some time to find models and ways of explaining goals and structures that resonated across constituencies. As had happened with assessment when it was first introduced, planners for the ADC were all trying to get buy-in for the new efforts in adult education, but we needed a wide range of metaphors and symbols to explain transformations.

I found myself drawing lots of pictures. For example, for the Access Pedagogy to work, faculty needed to determine how to shape their practice to a "porous walls" environment in their classes (i.e., be open to letting others in to see what was happening as a model for better learning and better teaching). In recruiting and training the learning coaches, we needed to find ways to refigure and explain the Vygotskian notion of a "more capable peer" to show that learning is accessible and to engage in sharing good practices in information management, applied technology skills, and critical reading rather than in "tutoring" for content. We came upon the habit of explaining the face-to-face work as "homework" that happens in "our house."

EM: One of the things that made this easier for me was my experience in experiential learning using community partners. I was accustomed to "giving up control" to the partnerships, and this was a similar experience in working in the ADC program. When working with a community partner, roles become blurred and students learn from each other, and from people who are not typically seen as teachers. Designing paired assignments with another faculty member was also hard to do, but I felt more primed to do that than many of my colleagues.

MW: Eric, you are a New Majority learner because your prior work in business and your concurrent volunteer work gave you a nontraditional academic's approach. You were open to an administrator with a fluid role. You were accustomed to budgeting and redesign in a way that was similar to what one does as an entrepreneur or in business. You were sufficiently unorthodox and I valued your experience in ways that contributed to the ADC program.

EM: My dissertation was on electricity deregulation. One of my early opportunities was to create a statewide education program on deregulation in New Jersey that would be delivered through Rutgers University. I arrived at my first "train-the-trainer" session. I had a big stack of transparency slides and was prepared to present them when a communication professor from Rutgers exclaimed, "Put those away! Don't you want them to learn anything?"

She told me to get people in groups and have them write down what they thought people would ask. That professor taught me an incredibly valuable lesson; students need to have an ownership stake in their learning. And without that, they are unlikely to learn much of anything. The need to understand and value what students bring into the classroom was a pivotal point for me.

MW: And, how to learn with others. Early in my career, I taught lunch-time classes at a military base. One of my favorite stories relates to a time when I was teaching a class and all of the students were much older than I was. Just out of graduate school, I was a bit puffed up with myself. Look at me, all "teachy."

Anyway, my class was on the factory floor, and for this particular lesson I was talking—always talking (I wish I could get refunds for my poor students back then)—about how to do research for their major paper assignment. The presentation was very traditional and focused on myself and the library search. In self-important reverie, I said, "My favorite thing in the whole world is to get a stack of books and articles, read them, and then look up the sources and read those too. I could spend all day in a good library doing just that."

A woman who was one of my more elderly students looked absolutely horrified and declared, "Honey, aren't you married? Don't you like sex?" Red-faced, I had no answer to this. I could no longer talk about how wonderful the research process was, as an exercise in romanticism, in the same way.

After a very good laugh at the incident, I started to ponder my authority and my identity. Eventually, these reflections and those wonderful learners on the base would lead to me think about how important *fit* is to eliminating fear of failure and of not belonging and to enhancing focus by articulating the value of the learning and the relevance of what and how we learn to students' lives and goals. This was and is a very personal issue with me as, raised in poverty with food and safety insecurity, I was drawn to education as a way to change my stars. From this, I began to wonder why people pursue education and what do they want to gain.

One example, continues to drive me. In a community college in Harrisburg, Pennsylvania, I had a student, Robbie, who would meet me at my office door and walk with me to class as he talked about his goals and aspirations. He would say, "I'm going to finish school and start a business and buy my mother a house." Then one day, he didn't show up. Exactly one year after 9/11, Robbie was killed going after someone who had robbed his girlfriend. He died alone in the street in the rain.

The next day, the older black women in the class asked the students to think about the example of Robbie and his lost opportunities. They began the class by lecturing the other students about how the young black men needed to change their lives to be successful because Robbie could not. These women continued as a cohort and became advocates for their educations as well as those of others. These are two moments in our intersected lives that made me see what I had not seen before and provided a key in my educational philosophy and behaviors that made me want to get the students to see who they are and who they could be.

EM: This reminds me of my experience with a former business partner who was an excellent sales person but hated sales pitches. He knew that "features and benefits" were not the main drivers of a sale. Instead he was focused on "pain," or why they are there and what they need. What is motivating the students? Why are they really here? Do they really care about it as much as I do?

MW: Maybe it is a way for them to grapple with the invisible value of learning. I like the way you bring practicality to the conversations about learning. We did not know what we needed when we started.

BS: *What you have learned about building relationships? What is needed to make cross-campus collaborations sustainable? What is the impact on new majority?*

MW: How important it is to have lots of people at the table from the beginning and to spend time not presenting but discussing how what you would be doing would impact others. Not assuming that you know what is going to work and how it will work. Because I learned to be more sensitive to others, I wanted to hear about their "pain points" and how it matters to have everyone at the table. There is something that is keeping them awake at night—wasted resources, academic integrity, etc. All those issues have to be considered, but the work still has to happen.

To create an environment, one voice can't dominate. Higher education is accustomed to accommodating everyone and shying away from things that are uncomfortable. Your institutional mission and vision must be the focus; you can't change your mission because it is the fixed foot of the compass. You can't go any farther than your mission can take you. Everyone at the table came because of the mission and you can't get away from that.

EM: It's so important to understand where people are coming from. How are they viewing and perceiving things? It could be fear of change, or the stress of having more work to do, or just the comfort of sailing along. One of things that you, Marguerite, helped me learn, see, and articulate in a different way, is that this is not "extra work" to redesign the learning environment. Some of the language you used and some of the language I use now is about how to make lives easier—students' lives easier and our work more impactful.

MW: The biggest thing I learned in developing the ADC is to talk about what faculty and staff love and what drives them to the work every day. Things are easier because they are more joyful. There are enough different people around the table to complete the work, and it is a design element now in my work to talk about the things that we love. The resolution of the pain point becomes the love object. Then we can ask them to think about how to think about the workplace that immerses people in what they love. They can give what they don't love to others who do love it.

One of the great hopes in transformational learning today is that the traditional classroom model of one professor and thirty students can be supplanted with asking them instead to concentrate on what is beautiful and urgent about their subject and letting others take on the related issues into the larger environment. I learned that from doing reflections before the meeting.

BS: *What are these reflections?*

MW: At Cabrini, before major meetings start, someone is asked to bring a text that centers people on the task—a poem, prayer, song, etc. The person making the presentation explains the link between the reflection and the purpose of the meeting. It was my favorite part of the culture. Just this simple act conveyed how we are linked by our values and our great hope for the institution. I've carried that practice to my new position at a public, urban community college. The settings couldn't be more different, but the passion for aligning work with values is a common thread, so centering on a reflection is a good fit for the work needed.

EM: My way of seeing this [cross-campus collaboration] is that there are some administrators who say they are going to shield the faculty and protect them from the world. But to me, being transparent about the business of the college is important. While defending academic freedom is important, it's also important for everyone to realize that higher education is a business. If we're not thinking about our customers, the market, and competition, one day we may have little left to defend.

MW: Adrienne Tinsley, former president of Bridgewater College, said, "Faculty love their subjects, but somebody has to love the institution." When I heard this, I thought I had found the best gold nugget to explain why I had left faculty work to the life of an administrator. It became a practiced trope I would use in job interviews. But Eric, in the New Majority institution, I have come to understand that the statement is not exactly right. In fact, everyone must love the institution—the specific institution we've committed ourselves to, to the institution of higher education, and to the larger society that makes a space for higher learning. As faculty, we show this love through our discipline. Our subject matter needs to be urgent in sustaining the institution.

I had never questioned Tinsley's quote until now, but it is not as much of a truism as it might seem today because the institution of higher education is under so many threats. The value of learning needs to be made visible, and everyone has to question everything.

EM: As one who contributes to the learning product (i.e., graduated students) I see that we can't remain in a bubble. I feel we are all capable of improving, but are we invited to contribute to the learning product? As a faculty member, am I invited to participate in the evolution of the institution and our product? And am I inviting the growing number of educational collaborators—staff, administrators, community members, alums, and others—to participate in this process as well?

BS: *How can we shape the learning environment that is needed for New Majority institutions to succeed?*

EM: Part of shaping a learning environment is how you recognize what people bring to class. In some classes, I rely on students to bring their knowledge (for example, of current technologies) into the class and make active contributions. And "personalized assignments," where students choose a topic or subject that has personal importance to them is one way of inviting and cultivating ownership. On a good day, the learning environment is inviting students to bring themselves, their experiences, opinions, fears, and doubts.

MW: My first thought is, question everything and weigh everything. I thought about Tim O'Brien's "The Things They Carried," a short story set in the Vietnam War. All the characters in the story have things that weigh them down, literally and figuratively, but as their marches continue through the jungles of Vietnam, they have to empty out their packs. The narrator recounts the exact weight of everything.

The metaphor is they are shedding the things they thought they needed, and at the crux of the story, a lieutenant considers a pebble he's been carrying because it represents romantic notions of a lost love. When he comes to the realization that his romantic notions make him less able to be vigilant for his troops, he throws the pebble away.

Within the New Majority conversation, we can see throwing things out of our backpacks as a metaphor for what students shed as they become new people. They drop them, but they also weigh the personal cost of the change. Relatedly, faculty members and administrators may be encouraged to shed what they carry to see things differently and do something new.

For example, it took a long time for me to stop leading with my own personal story of disadvantages and how they triggered my search for education because I thought it mattered in helping people on a similar journey connect to me as a teacher and as person. Now, I don't have time to tell my story because so much has changed in the academy, and it is gradually becoming more receptive to students with different points of origin in higher education. I don't feel the need to defend myself as one who took five years to complete the degree, while I worked as a secretary and a waitress, especially in the New Majority classroom.

BS: *What have you learned from being part of this book?*

EM: Working with Marguerite helped me see the academic transformation language as a way to improve what and how I do things. I don't need to feel shame in asking for help or calling upon the many support resources available on my campus. This has allowed me to focus most on what I am most passionate about, and open myself up to possibly better ways of doing things that I might not be as good at. It made me think about the world in a different way.

Another area is giving recognition—legitimacy—to things that I had already started to see and do for my students, before I even became aware of the idea New Majority students. When I read the literature on New Majority students, and what they need, it was very affirming in a way. I had instinctively found myself doing things that the emerging literature suggests. There is partial success and more to do, but it has been fun.

A third part, as an economist and business professor, it's given me a fresh reason to look at the fiscal resources of the campus. This has provided a context in which to think about the struggles faculty and students face, and translate those into economic models. It has become clear that the New Majority will be an important part of our university's future. As our programs grow, it will become increasingly important that people across campus know about the New Majority.

MW: When you are in leadership, you consider how you have a vision and how you attract stakeholders to work together to achieve it. In working on this project, I learned that although I had some knowledge in many of the areas because of the positions I've held, the book is better because it came from multiple voices. You have a complex picture that might have been oversimplified if only one person was addressing the issues. Taking the time to listen to the shared values has been very important. The authors show what the New Majority reflects, that expertise comes from the combination of or accumulated experience as well as training in the discipline.

I also learned that in trying to infer what people might have meant allowed me to bring a vision of the work that we need to do as a large text and think of how to integrate multiple perspectives. For example, you made me think of Tim O'Brien's story or John Donne's extended metaphor of the mission as the fixed foot that shows how we are more alike than we might realize. This reminds me that all workers in higher education bring their way of thinking about the world, and that way is centrally tied to our own academic disciplines. What's interesting about higher education administration is that we can come from different disciplines but be in the same administrative space.

BS: *What do you want to do now?*

EM: I am excited to help people engage in similar conversations and think about where an institution is going, who our students are, and how we can work together to meet their needs. This was an invitation to engage me as a faculty member in conversations about how we can be part of the big picture of student learning. I hope to have more of these conversations.

MW: Well, of course I'm ready to finish the next project we're working on together, a kind of companion book to this that provides additional cases as well as frameworks for carrying out projects to support New Majority learners.

However, I'm reflecting on how the president suggested that the work to build the ADC program for New Majority learners could not be successful if I didn't reach out to Eric and to other faculty influencers. Such wisdom in that. The key in being successful is to invite others to help, but it was framed as how can we cocreate this. I need to be open to thought partners who can help in maintaining the focus of educating the whole person and the total leadership approach to learning. It will be calamitous if higher ed[ucation] becomes too compartmentalized and it does not reach all. As a society, we are better when we are educated.

BS: *What are the risks? How is this professional development? What is to gain and lose in accepting the invitation?*

EM: It is usually less risky to stay in your office and not worry about politics or the broader health of the institution. But there is much to be said about working with others, to thoughtfully contributing to the future of an institution and to its effectiveness and being part of making something greater. As a tenured faculty member, the risks are lessened, but here are more human risks—rejection, the risk of people saying your ideas do not make sense, campus politics, and budgets. To be part of the process makes you accountable for the process and its success or failure. You use your political and personal capital to do things, and it may or may not work. That is life.

MW: When I started doing the work related to explaining patterns of retention that became the Fit-Fear-Focus model, there was safety in that because the people I talked to wanted a clear way to talk about what they think of as student experience. The model gives you a sense of satisfaction. But just when we think we have something true and essential, fate has a way of bringing the challenge of unexpected perspectives.

At an early conference with my new colleagues at Baltimore County Community College (BCCC), I was explaining Fit-Fear-Focus as a structure to support outcomes of belonging, security and hope in our students. Just then, a program director, with a look of concern expressed, "But many of our employees don't have belonging, security, and hope. What can we do for them so they have it to give to students?" I was leveled. Just as with the humorous event about research strategies on that factory floor, I was reminded that I can't be so self-certain and contained with these theories. What I hope I gain is a voice that encourages people to put down the book and do something.

References

Allen, Elaine, and Jeff Seaman. (2014). *Grade Change: Tracking Online Education in the United States*. Retrieved July 10, 2011, from http://www.onlinelearningsurvey.com/reports/gradechange.pdf

American Association of Colleges and Universities. (2013). *High Impact Practices*. Retrieved July 10, 2017, from https://www.aacu.org/resources/high-impact-practices

Atherton, J. S. (2013). *Learning and Teaching: Convergent and Divergent Learning*. Retrieved June 5, 2015, from http://www.learningandteaching.info/learning/converge.htm

Attewell, P., and Lavin, D. (2012). "The other 75%: College education beyond the elite." In E. C. Langemann, & H. Lewis (Eds.), *What Is College for? The Public Purpose of Higher Education*. New York: Teachers College, Columbia University.

Bar-On, Reuven. (1988). "The development of a concept of psychological well-being." Ph.D. diss., Rhodes University, South Africa.

Bar-On, Reuven. (2001). "Emotional intelligence and self-actualization." *Emotional Intelligence in Everyday Life: A Scientific Inquiry*: 82–97.

Barr, Margaret J., and George S. McClellan. (2011). *Budgets and Financial Management in Higher Education*, 2nd ed. Hoboken, NJ: John Wiley & Sons.

Bass, Randall. (2012). *Disrupting Ourselves: The Problem of Learning in Higher Education*. Retrieved July 10, 2017, from http://er.educause.edu/articles/2012/3/disrupting-ourselves-the-problem-of-learning-in-higher-education

Bowl, Marion. (2001). "Experiencing the barriers: Non-traditional students entering higher education." *Research Papers in Education* 16, no. 2: 141–160. doi: 10.1080/02671520110037410.

Bureau of Labor Statistics. (2017). *Number of Jobs Held in a Lifetime*. Retrieved July 10, 2017, from https://www.bls.gov/nls/nlsfaqs.htm#anch41

Caruso, David R., and Peter Salovey. (2004). *The Emotionally Intelligent Manager: How to Develop and Use the Four Key Emotional Skills of Leadership*. Hoboken, NJ: John Wiley & Sons.

Center for Engaged Learning. (n.d.). *Internships*. Retrieved October 4, 2016, from http://www.centerforengagedlearning.org/doing-engaged-learning/internships/#impact-practices

Center for Postsecondary and Economic Success. (2015). *Yesterday's Non-Traditional Student Is Today's Traditional Student*. Retrieved July 10, 2017, from http://www.clasp.org/resources-and-publications/publication-1/CPES-Nontraditional-students-pdf.pdf

Choy, Susan. (2001). *Nontraditional Undergraduates*. Retrieved July 10, 2017, from http://nces.ed.gov/pubs2002/2002012.pdf

Christensen, C. M., and Henry J. Eyring. (2011). *The Innovative University: Changing the DNA of Higher Education from t the Inside Out*. San Francisco, CA: Jossey-Bass.

Cleaver, Joanne. (2012). *The Career Lattice: Combat Brain Drain, Improve Company Culture, and Attract Top Talent*. New York: McGraw-Hill.

Community College of Baltimore County. (2015). "High Impact Practices." Workshop presented at the 7th Annual Maryland Association of Community Colleges (MACC) Completion Summit, November.

Cranton, Patricia. (1994). *Understanding and Promoting Transformative Learning: A Guide for Educators of Adults*. New York: John Wiley & Sons.

References

Desrochers, Donna M., and Steven Hurlburt. (2014). *Trends in College Spending 2011–2014: A Delta Data Update*. American Institutes for Research. Retrieved July 11, 2017, from http://www.deltacostproject.org/sites/default/files/products/Delta%20Cost_Trends%20College%20Spending%202001-2011_071414_rev.pdf

Dueben, Rebecca. (2015). *Faculty Attitudes Toward Assessment*. Retrieved July 11, 2017, from http://gradworks.umi.com/10/04/10043064.html

Education Policy Center. (2012). *Degreeless in Debt: What Happens to Borrowers Who Drop Out*. Retrieved July 10, 2017, from http://educationpolicy.air.org/publications/degreeless-debt-what-happens-borrowers-who-drop-out

Erisman, Wendy, and Patricia Steele. (2015). *Adult College Completion in the 21st Century: What We Know and What We Don't*. Retrieved July 11, 2017, from https://higheredinsight.files.wordpress.com/2015/06/adult_college_completion_20151.pdf

Fain, Paul. (2012). *Hour by Hour*. Retrieved July 11, 2017, from https://www.insidehighered.com/news/2012/09/05/credit-hour-causes-many-higher-educations-problems-report-finds

Federal Student Aid. (n.d.). *Staying Eligible*. Retrieved July 11, 2017, from https://studentaid.ed.gov/sa/eligibility/staying-eligible

Finley, A., and McNair, T. (2013). *Assessing Underserved Students' Engagement in High Impact Practices*. Washington, DC: American Association of Colleges and Universities.

Fortni, Amy Ann, and Rob van der Meulen. (2016). *Gartner's 2016 Hype Cycle for Emerging Technologies Identifies Three Trends That Organizations Must Track to Gain Competitive Advantage*. Retrieved July 10, 2017, from http://www.gartner.com/newsroom/id/3412017

Friedman, Jordan. (2015). "Decide between online, blended courses." *U.S. News & World Report*. Retrieved July 10, 2017, from http://www.usnews.com/education/online-education/articles/2015/03/04/decide-between-online-blended-courses

Gaff, Jerry G. (2004). "What is a generally educated person?" *Peer Review*, 7, no. 1. Retrieved July 11, 2017, from https://www.aacu.org/publications-research/periodicals/what-generally-educated-person

Gogos, Roberta. (2014). *Why Blended Learning Is Better*. Retrieved July 11, 2017, from https://elearningindustry.com/why-blended-learning-is-better.

Goleman, Daniel P. (1995). *Emotional Intelligence: Why It Can Matter More Than IQ for Character, Health and Lifelong Achievement*. New York: Bantam Books.

Goleman, Daniel. (2015). "What makes a leader?"

Graham, Charles R., Stephanie Allen, and Donna Ure. (2005). "Benefits and challenges of blended learning environments." In *Encyclopedia of Information Science and Technology* (pp. 253–259). Hershey, PA: IRMA.

Habley, W. R., J. L. Bloom, and S. Robbins. (2012). *Increasing Persistence: Research-Based Strategies for College Student Success*. San Francisco, CA: Jossey-Bass.

Hanover Research. (2012). *6 Alternative Budget Models for Colleges and Universities*. Retrieved October 4, 2016, from http://www.hanoverresearch.com/2012/04/02/6-alternative-budget-models-for-colleges-and-universities/

Hardin, Garrett. (1968). "The Tragedy of the Commons." *Science* 162, no. 3859: 1243–1248.

Horizon Report. (2016). *2016 Higher Education Report*. Retrieved July 10, 2017, from http://cdn.nmc.org/media/2016-nmc-horizon-report-he-EN.pdf

Horton, Joann. 2015. "Identifying at-risk factors that affect college student success." *International Journal of Process Education*, 7, no. 1. Retrieved July 10, 2017, from http://www.processeducation.org/ijpe/2015/risk.pdf

Hummell, John D. (2012). *Financing Higher Education: Approaches to Funding at Four Year Public Institutions*. Ohio University Center for Higher Education working paper series. Retrieved July 11, 2017, from https://www.ohio.edu/education/centers-and-partnerships/centers/center-for-higher-education/loader.cfm?csModule=security/getfile&PageID=2149085

Kahneman, D. (2011). *Thinking, Fast and Slow*. New York, NY: Farrar, Straus & Giroux.

Kanfer, Ruth, Gilad Chen, and Robert D. Pritchard, eds. (2012). *Work Motivation: Past, Present and Future*. New York: Routledge.

Klenke, Karin. (2002). "Cinderella stories of women leaders: Connecting leadership contexts and competencies." *Journal of Leadership & Organizational Studies* 9, no. 2: 18–28.

Knowles, Malcolm. (1980). *The Modern Practice of Adult Education: Andragogy versus Pedagogy*. Englewood Cliffs, NJ: Prentice Hall/Cambridge.

Kuh, George D. (2008). *High-Impact Educational Practices: What They Are, Who Has Access to Them, and Why They Matter*. Washington, DC: American Association of Colleges and Universities.

Massey, William F., ed. (1996). *Resource Allocation in Higher Education*. Ann Arbor: University of Michigan Press.

Massey, William F. (2016). *Reengineering the University: How to Be Mission Centered, Market Smart, and Margin Conscious*. Baltimore: Johns Hopkins University Press.

Mayer, John D. & Peter Salovey. (1997). "What is emotional intelligence." In P. Salovey. & D. Sluyter (Eds.), *Emotional Development and Emotional Intelligence: Educational Implications* (pp. 3–34). New York: HarperCollins.

Mayer, John D., Peter Salovey, David R. Caruso, and Gill Sitarenios. (2001). "Emotional intelligence as a standard intelligence." *Emotion* 1, no. 3: 232–242.

McClelland, David C. (1973). "Testing for competence rather than for intelligence." *American Psychologist* 28, no. 1: 1–14.

McDonnell, Peter, ed. (2016). *The Experiential Library: Transforming Academic and Research Libraries through the Power of Experiential Library*. Cambridge, UK: Chandros Publishing.

National Center for Education Statistics. (n.d.). *National Postsecondary Student Aid Study—Overview*. Retrieved April 25, 2017, from https://nces.ed.gov/surveys/npsas/.

National Center for Education Statistics. (2014). *Digest of Education Statistics, 2014 Tables*. Retrieved July 10, 2017, from: https://nces.ed.gov/programs/digest/d14/tables/dt14_303.40.asp

National Center for Education Statistics. (2015). *College Student Employment*. Retrieved from. http://nces.ed.gov/programs/coe/indicator_ssa.asp

National Center for Educational Statistics. (2016). *Characteristics of Postsecondary Students*. Retrieved July 10, 2017, from https://nces.ed.gov/programs/coe/indicator_csb.asp

National Center for Education Statistics. (2016). *Fast Facts: Graduation Rates*. Retrieved July 11, 2017, from https://nces.ed.gov/fastfacts/display.asp?id=40

National Center for Education Statistics. (2016). *PowerStat Data Retrieval Tool*. Retrieved from https://nces.ed.gov/datalab/powerstats/default.aspx

National Center for Education Statistics. (2016). *Fast Facts: Tuition Costs of Colleges and Universities*. Retrieved July 11, 2017, from https://nces.ed.gov/fastfacts/display.asp?id=76

National Student Clearinghouse. (2012). *More Than One-Third of College Students Are over 25*. Retrieved July 11, 2017, from http://www.studentclearinghouse.org/about/media_center/press_releases/files/release_2012-04-19.pdf

National Student Clearinghouse Research Center. (2014). *Some College, No Degree: A National View of Students with Some College Enrollment, But No Completion*. Retrieved July 10, 2017, from https://nscresearchcenter.org/signaturereport7/

National Survey of Student Engagement (NSSE). (2016). *Engagement Indicators and High-Impact Practices*. Retrieved July 11, 2017, from http://nsse.indiana.edu/html/engagement_indicators.cfm

Ninon, Sonia. (2013). *Non-Returning Students Survey Results*. Indianapolis, IN: Ivy Technical College. Retrieved July 10, 2017, from https://www.ivytech.edu/files/IR__13161_Non-Returning_Student_Survey_Results_Final.pdf

Online Learning Consortium. (2015). *2015 Online Report Card: Tracking Online Education in the United States*. Available at https://onlinelearningconsortium.org/read/online-report-card-tracking-online-education-united-states-2015/

References

Osborn, Richard. (2008). Unlocking the Transformational Power of Continuing Education. 70th Annual Conference and Meeting Proceedings: 6–7. Retrieved April 25, 2017, from http://www.acheinc.org/Resources/Documents/Proceedings/2008_proceedings.pdf

Penn State University. *Online Faculty Development.* Retrieved April 25, 2017. http://wcfd.psu.edu/programs/courses/

Pines, Ayala M., Margaret B. Neal, Leslie B. Hammer, and Tamar Icekson. (2011). "Job burnout and couple burnout in dual-earner couples in the sandwiched generation." *Social Psychology Quarterly* 74, no. 4: 361–386. doi:10.1177/0190272511422452.

Pugh, Michael. (2013). *Dropping Out Means Paying Back Financial Aid.* Retrieved July 11. 2017, from http://www.fastweb.com/financial-aid/articles/dropping-out-means-paying-back-financial-aid

Rubin, Beth. (2013). "University Business Models and Online Practices: A Third Way." *Online Journal of Distance and Learning Administration* 16, no. 1. Available at http://www.westga.edu/~distance/ojdla/spring161/rubin.html

Salovey, Peter, and John D. Mayer. (1990). "Emotional intelligence." *Imagination, Cognition and Personality* 9, no. 3: 185–211.

Serna, Gabriela R., and Spencer C. Weiler. (2016). *Higher Education, Fiscal Administration, and Budgeting An Applied Approach.* Lanham, MD: Rowman & Littlefield.

Shumski, Daniel. (2011). *Five Failed Start-Ups You Should Study.* Retrieved July 10, 2017, from http://www.educationdive.com/news/5-failed-education-startups-you-should-study/196134/

Smith, Peter. (2008). *The Quiet Crisis: How Higher Education Is Failing America.* San Francisco, CA: Jossey-Bass.

Soares, Louise. (2013). *Post-traditional Learners and the Transformation of Postsecondary Education: A Manifesto for College Leaders.* American Council on Education. Retrieved July 10, 2017, from http://www.acenet.edu/news-room/Documents/Post-traditional-Learners.pdf

US Department of Education. (2015). *Demographic and Enrollment Characteristics of Nontraditional Undergraduates: 2011–12.* Retrieved July 10, 2017, from https://nces.ed.gov/pubs2015/2015025.pdf

Weber, Marguerite. (2014). "Design for student success: lessons learned, continuous improvements needed." In *2014 Sourcebook.* Consortium for Student Retention Data Exchange. Norma, OK: University of Oklahoma Press.

Weber, Marguerite. (2015). "Promoting adult learner success through adapted high impact practices." In *2015 Sourcebook.* Consortium for Student Retention Data Exchange. Norman, OK: University of Oklahoma Press.

Wonacott, Michael. (2001). *Adult Students: Recruitment and Retention.* ERIC Clearinghouse on Adult and Career and Vocational Education. Practice Application Brief, no. 18. Retrieved April 25, 2017, from www. http://eric.ed.gov/?id=ED457405.

Zak, Paul. (2013). *Measurement Myopia.* Retrieved July 10, 2017, from http://www.druckerinstitute.com/2013/07/measurement-myopia/

About the Editors

Eric Malm is an associate professor of economics and business management at Cabrini University in Radnor, Pennsylvania. He provides the framework for understanding the New Majority as a specific group of learners. He has developed experiential hybrid classes, started his own marketing companies, and has created policies and led training sessions on the role of technology in teaching and learning. Here, he outlines the demographic and traces the characteristics and needs of New Majority learners to open the way for exploring other issues addressed in this volume.

Marguerite Weber is vice president for student affairs at Baltimore County Community College and has focused the majority of her professional career on both the learning needs of adult students and on the structures of higher education in designing appropriately flexible learning environments. She has served as the vice president for adult and professional programs at Cabrini University, been the academic innovation fellow for the University System of Maryland, and has held teaching and administrative positions in Maryland, New York, and Pennsylvania. Her learning design, called the Fit/Fear/Focus Model, is discussed as a way to engage students to persist as well as a vision for organizing the higher-education infrastructures to support diverse learners as they strive to achieve success.

About the Contributors

William A. Egan is an instructional designer for Penn State University's World Campus, where he specializes in designing and developing effective instruction for online and hybrid learning environments for a variety of graduate and undergraduate disciplines. Since 1998, the World Campus has offered unique value for adult learners, members of the military, and corporations seeking opportunities to increase workforce training and development. But the flexibility of online learning makes it an increasingly attractive option for students in the New Majority as well. In chapter 6, he offers best practices for effective program design and decision making for faculty, IT professionals, instructional designers, and administrators that will enable them to create programs and courses that are appropriately structured and sequenced, clearly communicated, and accessible to a variety of users with differing learning needs.

Patricia Griffin is the director of adult programs at Cabrini University in Radnor, Pennsylvania. Drawing from her previous work at Boston College and St. Joseph's University in Philadelphia, Pennsylvania, Griffin examines from practitioner–theorist perspective what it means for institutions to be student centered, for faculty to be adaptive in their pedagogy, and how curricular innovation may influence students' perceptions of their abilities to persist to degree completion.

Beverly Schneller, associate provost for academic affairs at Belmont University in Nashville, Tennessee, is also a Teagle Assessment Scholar with the Center of Inquiry at Wabash College in Crawfordsville, Indiana. In addition to writing and publishing on literary topics and assessment of student learning, she is a consultant to colleges and universities on topics ranging from writing across the curriculum design and assessment to developing programs and curricula to enhance diversity.

Ayisha Sereni provides the voice of a New Majority learner and a success story in her journey from Montgomery County Community College to Drexel University in Pennsylvania to her MBA at the University of Scranton. She is currently a PhD candidate at Eastern University in organizational leadership. Her essay focuses on her diverse experiences as a student and as the Associate Dean of Academic Affairs at Harrisburg Area Community College in Harrisburg, Pennsylvania, with a special emphasis on what did and did not work for her as she transitioned from being a student to being an academic leader. Sereni is now president of the Main Line School of Real Estate.

Paul Walsh, USMx project director at University System of Maryland, has been engaged in teaching with technology and in faculty professional development as an instructional designer since 1987. In chapter 5, he takes a closer look at what it means to say students, and particularly New Majority students, are digital natives and how that translates into the higher-education environment of today.

Made in the USA
Middletown, DE
24 October 2017